S0-DON-749

SURVIVING MINISTRY

SURVIVING MINISTRY

Ronald D. Sisk

SMYTH & HELWYS
PUBLISHING, INC.

ISBN 1-880837-48-X

Surviving Ministry

Ronald D. Sisk

Copyright © 1997
Smyth & Helwys Publishing, Inc.®
6316 Peake Road
Macon, Georgia 31210-3960
1-800-568-1248

All rights reserved.
Printed in the United States of America.

The paper used in this publication meets the minimum
requirements of American Standard for Information
Sciences–Permanence of paper for Printed Library
Materials, ANSI Z39.48–1984.

Library of Congress Cataloging-in-Publication Data

Sisk, Ronald D.
       Surviving ministry / Ronald D. Sisk
       viii + 184pp.   6" x 9" (15 x 23 cm.)
       Includes bibliographical references.
       ISBN 1-880837-48-X   (alk. paper)
       1. Clergy-Professional ethics.
       2. Clergy-Office.
       I. Title.
       BV4011.5.S57
       241'.641-dc20   1997   96-34104
                                                                                    CIP

CONTENTS

PART 2
THE PUBLIC SPHERE
Problems of the Minister's Life in Professional Practice

PREFACE

Most training programs for ministers major on academic preparation for ministry, biblical studies, church history, systematic theology, and so on. While practical preparation has become much more important in recent years, there is still, in most instances, very little time given to the minister's personal and professional ethical formation. Ministers are left to learn by trial and error—mostly error—once they are in the parish situation itself.

As a trained ethicist and a minister for nearly two decades, in this book I draw on my experience to provide students, ministers in practice, and lay church leaders with a systematic, concrete, case-assisted approach to the ethics of ministry. Most of this volume applies equally well to ministers in a broad range of staff positions. While I write from my own perspective as a Baptist (we must all start someplace!), the principles developed herein are intended for an ecumenical audience. The dynamics of parish life remain remarkably similar across doctrinal lines.

Methodology is quite simple. Within the two broad categories of the minister's personal and professional life, I analyze six of the most critical issue areas of ministry:

Vocation
Spirituality
Stewardship
Authority
Shepherding
Prophecy

Within each category, I identify critical questions the minister must address. For instance,

How do you balance family life and ministry?
How much money can you ask for?
What if someone brings an AIDS baby to the church nursery?
Is there a right time to leave the ministry?

For each question we consider an evocative case study, examine how the issue has been addressed in the church historically, apply appropriate biblical teachings, and develop a set of applicable principles.

The overall intent is to set forth a sound theological and ethical framework for the practice of ministry that ministers may use themselves in day-to-day work, and to suggest a decision-making method that may be used to address new ministerial issues as they arise. I speak of real life events and specific experiences of my own ministry precisely because it is in the context of such real life experiences that ministry must be lived.

Speaking of real life, special thanks go to my wife Sheryl, who keeps me honest in balancing personal and professional commitments; to our son Douglas, whose zest for life surrounds me every time I walk through the door; and to the people who have done me the great honor of allowing me to be their minister.

Part 1
The Private Sphere

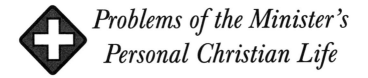

*Problems of the Minister's
Personal Christian Life*

CHAPTER 1

VOCATION

Before you are a minister, you are a person, a child of God. That you become a minister is the result of your perception of God's leadership in your life. Roman Catholics have called it "having a vocation" for the ministry. But how does that leadership come? How do you know when it is compelling? How do you work it out in the context of an individual Christian life? These are the ethical issues of ministerial vocation.

How do I receive my call?

My home pastor swears he heard an audible voice. He gets a kind of half-apologetic look on his face and tells of riding in the car to church as a teenager and hearing, apparently from nowhere, a voice in his ear saying, "Luke 4:18." He was not well-schooled enough in scripture to catch the reference immediately; but from the moment he disovered that it was Jesus' description of *his* own call, my friend was absolutely certain God had called him to ministry. He has now quite happily served most of a lifetime, in circumstances often less than ideal. And his memory of that experience and its effect is no less vivid today than the day it happened.

My own experience was no less memorable, if somewhat less dramatic. As in many evangelical churches, the congregation in which I grew up boasted one elderly woman identified by all as "the saint" of the church. Grandma Nonie, ancient, arthritic, nearly blind, nonetheless exuded the joy of the faith. One Sunday evening when I was about fourteen, she caught my hand in the aisle of the sanctuary after worship and said, "Ronnie, God has something for you to do." It was more than a decade before I decided to enter the ministry, but from that moment I knew I was called.

What are the historical models for a call to the ministry?

In some ways each of these two experiences exemplifies the way calling has been experienced in the church. Sometimes it has been a profound experience of the individual. Sometimes it has come through the fellowship of the church. Both of these methods of legitimate calling are found in history and scripture, along with a third we shall discuss shortly. In addition, of course, there are more than a few examples of illegitimate calling and of illegitimate responses to a genuine call. There are also more than a few examples of the personal and social havoc wreaked both by ministers not truly called of God and by those who have responded unworthily to God's call. Obviously the question of what exactly a "calling" is and how it is experienced requires careful explication.

As early as Tertullian in A.D. 208, the church had begun to draw a distinction between the clergy (*kleros*, "called") and laity (*laos*, "people or crowd").[1] That distinction became more and more pronounced with the flowering of Roman Catholicism and its high view of the priesthood and of the monastic life. The common people or laity were held to be incapable of completely pleasing God within the context of everyday life. True piety demanded separation from the sensual confines of marriage and the common contamination of daily business. Thus the clergy came to hold a position not only of a different function within the church but also of a different quality of relationship with God. This special priestly relationship to God became a foundational idea in both the theology and ecclesiology of Catholicism. The church became a hierarchy in which the priests were set apart by ordination to a holy life. Having received a mystic call from God, a layperson would become a candidate for ordination to the priesthood.

In ordination, a priest received from his superiors a special blessing that they in turn had received when they were ordained. The concept of "apostolic succession" traced this blessing back through the years to Christ's choice of the twelve and the particular primacy of Peter. As Peter's successors, the priests mediated the grace of Christ to the common people. The church, linked by this priestly succession, was thus an organic unity, held together not only by the power of the Spirit but also by the physical/mystical transmission of that Spirit from priest to priest through the ages by the laying on of hands. The mystical power of this idea makes it easy to see why ordination has gained such a hold on the Christian imagination that even denominations such as the Baptists whose theology emphasizes the priesthood of the believer still hold to the practice.

In fact, with the exception of the Quakers, all the churches of the Reformation have retained some idea of the importance of calling and setting aside clergy to the task of ministry within the church. They alter it radically, however, from the Roman concept of the priesthood.

In his tract *To the Christian Nobility of the German Nation Regarding the Reform of the Christian Estate*, Martin Luther demolished the idea of the priesthood as a separate and holy class set apart from the laity by ordination.

> The pope or bishop anoints, shaves heads, ordains, consecrates, and prescribes garb different from that of the laity, but he can never make a man into a Christian or into a spiritual man by so doing. As far as that goes, we are all consecrated priests through baptism.[2]

For Luther, the church itself should call its priests.

> It should be the custom for every town to choose from among the congregations a learned and pious citizen, entrust to him the office of the ministry, and support him at the expense of the congregation.[3]

By making the ministry an office, Luther suggested that, given the right circumstances, any Christian may perform the duties of a minister. Ministry becomes simply another function necessary for the well-being of the church. It loses much of its mystical aura.

With the rise of nationalism in Europe, high-church Protestantism took the demystification of the clerical calling a step further by tying ministerial appointments to the mechanisms of the state. In England, appointment as the vicar of a parish was often in the hands of the local landowner or of some representative of the king. Ministry often became a profession one chose for social or financial advantage rather than a way of life that chose the individual. This is not to say that ministry as a profession is somehow suspect.

As Gaylord Noyce suggests regarding the Latin root of the term professional, "The most common early use relates to making a vow, as by monks entering upon their order."[4] The modern professional model of the ministry, which is our third legitimate model for calling, differs from the other two in the emphasis placed on the rational choice of the individual. Noyce provides an excellent brief discussion of the tension in the mainline understanding of ministry between the concepts of profession and calling. He ends by suggesting it is both, without really dealing with the perceived difference in how one enters the ministry in the first place.

In most American communities, at least until the mid-twentieth century, ministers of the mainline established churches were educated professionals, often the most educated men [almost always men] in town. While many, indeed most, of these men were no less devout than those called to preach in frontier revivals, the process of calling was for them very different. A desire to help people and a love for the life of the mind and the spirit, rather than an "irrational" call, became the accepted criteria for entering the ministry in the mainline church. Though always considered a bit suspect by evangelicals and perhaps also by Catholics, this professional model came to dominate much of American Protestantism in general and theological education in particular.

While there was always a pietistic streak in English Christianity (witness the seventeenth-century exodus to America as well as more establishment indicators such as William Law's *A Serious Call to a Devout and Holy Life*), the evangelical revivals of the eighteenth and nineteenth centuries made the "call to preach" an enduring force in American church life. Baptists, particularly, felt little need for an educated "professional" clergy in their backwoods cabins and brush arbors. The "call," felt by the individual and confirmed by the congregation, became the only criterion for entry into the pulpit.

The Anglicans, the Presbyterians, and even the Methodists quickly developed and enforced educational standards for their clergy. The founding documents of Harvard College declared the dread of "an illiterate ministry."[5] The Baptist founding of Brown University, however, was belied by a polity that prevented central regulation and a religious culture that largely valued experience above education. Even 200 years later, anti-intellectualism remains a powerful force in Baptist life.

We are left, then, with three models for the call to ministry that have operated historically within the church: (1) the mystical, "burning-bush," "Damascus road" experience of Moses and Paul; (2) the "calling out the called" experience of Ambrose and John Knox and this author; and (3) the professional choice made by devout folk through the ages whose minds and hearts simply told them the ministry was where they should be.

What are the biblical models for a call to the ministry?

The Scriptures are full of examples of God calling individuals and groups to specific tasks. Indeed, in one reading, that is what the Scriptures are, the written record of God's call to humankind to be about God's business.

One need go no further than the Garden to find the first biblical examples of God's direct, specific call to individuals. Giving Adam the task of naming the beasts and of caring for the Garden and giving Eve the task of serving as a "suitable companion" are no less than God's first essays into directing human vocation. One need only name the calls of Abraham, Moses, Isaiah, and Jeremiah to display plenty of Old Testament evidence for our first model of calling, that of an overt, individually perceived challenge from God.

Clearly from the earliest days the worshiping community believed that such a call was possible. As the exiled shepherd Moses walked the wilderness of Sinai caring for his sheep, God could speak from the eternal flame of a burning bush and alter his life purpose from that moment forward. In the high ecstasy of worship in the temple, God could open the mouth of Isaiah and make him a prophet to speak God's truth to Israel. Shepherd boys, dressers of sycamore trees, and queens of Persia found their lives changed forever as part of God's plan for God's people.

It is in this context of Hebrew faith that the New Testament continues the tradition of calling. K. L. Schmidt wrote,

> If Jesus does the calling in the Gospels, he does so in fulfillment of a divine function, and the proper response is faith, which carries with it not only discipleship but also the blessings of salvation. Behind the term [*kaleo*], then, stands the whole work of God through Christ, in judgment and grace.[6]

In other words, God's call to humankind to carry out God's purposes on earth is what the gospel is all about. As Henlee Barnette argues, every Christian is called to ministry.[7]

Still it is the specific call to vocational ministry that concerns us here. No more dramatic instance of the calling of an individual to vocational ministry exists than that of the Damascus road experience of Paul in Acts 9. Paul's calling contains elements that are often seen in this type of direct call. Initially the individual is pursuing his or her own direction, oblivious of or even hostile to the purposes of God. There is a numinous event, an encounter of some kind with the Spirit, which gives a radically new direction and purpose to life. Very often this experience of calling is so persuasive as to provide the unquestioned motivation for a lifetime of service. Jesus called Paul, and Paul's response changed the course of Christian history.

Similarly, scripture provides ample background for the practice of "calling out the called." God's choice of Saul and David as kings was conveyed to them, not by the direct intervention of the Spirit, but through the agency of Samuel. According to Acts 2, the "body of the disciples" was asked to choose the seven who would serve as deacons. They did so and the seven entered into service in answer to the call of the congregation. Paul charged Titus to choose elders for the churches of Crete and gave him the criteria for his choice, just as he had done for Timothy at Ephesus. Clearly, the church of the New Testament assumed both that the choices of the Spirit might be conveyed through human agency and that those callings must be honored by the ones called.

Our third model, that of the "professional" minister, takes its origin from the biblical institution of the priesthood. Initiated when God set apart Aaron and his sons in Exodus 28, the priesthood in Israel became a hereditary function of the tribe of Levi. Only Levites could be priests. Obviously, there is a profound difference between someone who inherits a role and someone who chooses to adopt a role at the impetus of the Holy Spirit. Just as clearly, there were many priests in Israel who chose to perform their inherited duties faithfully and well. The point here is that from the earliest days there have been those who came to the ministry in a natural kind of way just as the sons of an electrician might find that craft a natural choice for themselves.

To approach the problem from a slightly different angle, the Protestant emphasis on the doctrine of the priesthood of the believer creates a situation in which the choice of the vocational ministry simply allows a few Christians to choose to make their living at the tasks that are the calling of all. Peter argued:

> But you are a chosen race, a royal priesthood, a holy nation, God's own people, in order that you may proclaim the mighty acts of him who called you out of darkness into his marvelous light. (1 Pet 2:9)

All Christians are part of this new people. Therefore, all Christians are called as ministers whether they serve in a professional capacity or not. As Barnette concludes,

> Every Christian is called to be a minister regardless of how he earns his daily bread. Whether work be church-related or factory-related, the Christian is to remain faithful to the calling of God. Each has a grace gift to be exercised in the service of God and for the common good of the community.[8]

Even so, the biblical call is most often a specific call of a specific individual to a specific task, for example, "Set apart for me Barnabas and Saul for the work to which I have called them" (Acts 13:2). We are left with the questions of how one experiences such a call today and how one knows such an experience to be valid.

How is a call to the vocational ministry experienced and validated today?

The three historical and biblical models for a call to the vocational Christian ministry that we have surveyed are not usually experienced in an individual's life as separate and distinct paths. Most often, the three are intertwined. Persons with a deep devotion to God and an interest in service may find themselves moved by a particular experience of the Spirit to look at a Christian vocation for the first time. I very much doubt that the audible voice in the car was the first impetus of the Spirit toward ministry that my home pastor felt. More likely his family's devotion, his own religious training and experience, and a natural interest in service brought him to the point at which he could hear God's call when it came.

Certainly in my own life Grandma Nonie's announcement that I was called did not break into my awareness as an isolated shock. It came, in fact, on an evening when I had just completed a long personal spiritual struggle by giving myself to the Lord publicly in a new way in accordance with my church's practice. The people of Milan did not demand that Ambrose become their bishop on a moment's whim. Nor did John Bunyan's congregation confirm his call to preach without observing him exercise his gift again and again.

What we might suggest, then, is a threefold typology for evaluating and validating the individual call to ministers. First, ask the question, "Do they have a personal experience of the Spirit's impetus toward vocational ministry?" Have they experienced a call? No one, of course, can say with absolute certainty whether or not someone else's spiritual experience is valid. To evaluate this in a pietist or evangelical context is particularly difficult.

Too often conservatives interpret any call to greater devotion as a specific call to the vocational ministry. One young man of my acquaintance made it all the way into graduate theological study before he realized his true vocation was working with computers rather than church members. Another became a minister of education, even though some of his friends were convinced he would make a much better zoologist.

The second question helps us begin to deal with this problem of individual misperception of the divine will. Ask, "Does their faith community believe God's call to vocational ministry is legitimate for them?" Baptists, with their strong emphasis on local church autonomy, have traditionally been willing to educate for the ministry any individual whose home church would recommend them. A kind of weeding-out process takes place when some of those educated cannot find actual jobs in the ministry. In effect, the broader faith community rejects or redirects their call. A second level of weeding-out occurs in the first few years of ministry itself as some discover they are not temperamentally suited or appropriately talented for actual work in the parish.

Mainline Protestants and Roman Catholics, on the other hand, have tended to use somewhat more objective evaluations of a person's skills, delaying ordination till the candidate can demonstrate certain minimal ministerial skills. Ordination then conveys not only the affirmation of the congregation but a denominational affirmation of competence.

The third evaluative question to ask of potential ministers is this: "Do they want to do this? Do they enter the ministry freely and without significant reservation, as the way they wish to spend their professional life?" Notice that we here return to Noyce's concept of the profession of ministry as a way of life that one chooses. A neighbor pastor used to tell me repeatedly that he never wanted to be a minister in the first place. He claimed that he answered an irresistible call of God but remained as he had been from the beginning, miserable in his work.

Something is profoundly wrong in such a situation. Yes, there are ample instances of giants of the faith being called to the ministry by God and the community against their initial will. There are many reports of occasions when the desire to be Christ's minister faded or was temporarily eclipsed along the way. But to say that God calls anyone to a life of deliberate misery in a vocation with which they are not and cannot be comfortable is to deny God's nature as loving Parent. My miserable pastor friend either seriously misperceived God's intention for him or became stuck in a tragic, perennial rebellion. God does not call anyone to deliberate misery in any vocation.

The most easily validated call to the vocational ministry is thus initiated by one's own relationship with God. It is confirmed as the faith community sees in that individual a gift for ministry and allows that person the opportunity to exercise that gift in specific settings. And it is freely chosen as a result of the individual's own inclination and ability.

Such a choice is "professional" in the sense that it is voluntarily and deliberately elected in response to God's call. It may be "professional" in the sense of adhering to an objective set of standards for the adequate performance of ministry. Seen in this way, there is no substantive difference between the ministry's qualification as a profession and that of vocations such as law and medicine.

How do I choose a job in ministry?

Eleanor left the interview room furious. She knew it was about to happen again. Once more, for the seventh time in three years, a pastor selection committee was about to turn her down because she was a woman. As she got into the car to drive back across town to work, she found herself agonizing again about the associate ministry position she held in the little church on the wrong side of the tracks.

Some women, Eleanor knew, would have been ecstatic to have her ministry opportunity. The blue-collar, racially mixed neighborhood around her church was a gold mine of human needs. Eleanor's job description gave her primary responsibility for leading the congregation in carrying out community outreach programs. But Eleanor had never wanted that kind of position in the first place. She wanted to preach. She'd taken award after award for her pulpit work in seminary. She'd assumed that her ability would open the way to an educated congregation that could both appreciate and grow from her efforts.

She hadn't reckoned on the tradition that still, except in the rarest instances, kept women out of senior pastorates in her denomination. She knew she could do it! But as she parked behind the shabby building and went down the steps to the church basement to get things ready for that day's after school program, she found herself wondering if she'd ever get the chance.

To what extent historically has a call to the ministry been specific as opposed to general?

For the remainder of this chapter we will operate at the intersection between the concepts of the ministry as a calling and the ministry as a profession. Biblical descriptions of callings tended to be not only compelling but specific. One can hardly imagine the apostle Paul reconsidering whether he wanted to take the gospel to the Gentiles or become pastor of First Church Jerusalem.

Modern ministries tend very often to be both less specific and less enduring. Preparation for ministry today requires more than a fire in the belly. And someone who begins with that particular hunger to serve the poor in Appalachia or grow a yuppie congregation on the edge of the Washington Beltway may well find that getting there follows a much longer and more circuitous route than they had anticipated.

In most denominations it means obtaining a bachelor's degree in some liberal arts subject, followed by at least three years of seminary training and possibly more. There are internships to be served, examinations to be passed, and credentials to be obtained. As with any profession, there are "entry-level" positions and churches, and there are those that normally require experience and a certain standing among one's colleagues and denomination. Then, like Eleanor, one may find oneself hindered by social conditions or prejudices quite beyond personal control. Thoughtful persons starting down the road toward a ministerial career may thus find themselves asking, "How and when can I get where I feel the Lord is calling me?" "Is my call to ministry in general or only to the specific field of service intriguing me now?"

Henlee Barnette used to say that the call of God for any person is to be found at the intersection of that person's ability and opportunities. The church early developed a catechuminal system by which those who wished to become full members attended a series of classes and had their behavior observed for as long as three years before they were permitted to be baptized. A similar kind of care was exercised for those who wished to enter the ministry.

By the third century, the church had developed a three-tiered system of clerical service. In every city the head of the church was the bishop. Bishops in the early days were elected locally from among the second tier, the presbyters. While bishops were both administrative and sacerdotal officers, presbyters often carried out the preaching and worship duties in a particular congregation. The deacons, who in the east could be male or female, assisted in caring for the physical needs of the congregation.[9]

There was always a kind of professional progression within this system. A deacon might with diligence and application aspire to become a presbyter. Presbyters formed the pool from which a new bishop was elected when a vacancy occurred. In that sense, the church's ministry structure quickly became hierarchical and rather rigid. Monasticism grew in part as a kind of broad-based response to the systematization of the church. By the sixth century, monasticism had moved from an almost exclusively lay beginning to provide an alternative route of advancement within the clergy. The rule and discipline of monastic life captured the popular imagination. Pope Gregory I was able to move from a monastery to become the head of the church of Rome.[10]

The acceptance of the church by Constantine began a long process of secularization of the choice of clergy. As nation-states grew in medieval Europe, it became common for the king's consent to be required for the selection of a bishop. In local parishes, the individual landowner might wield considerable influence in the selection of the vicar or parish priest. Throughout the Middle Ages, church and state struggled for influence in the selection and advancement of clergy.[11] By the modern era, even Cardinal Richelieu might still begin his service with a simple spiritual call to ministry, but the intertwining of the mechanisms of church and state seemed to have done at least as much to make the church secular as to make the state Christian.

The rise of universities and the status of theology as "the queen of the sciences" added the element of extensive education as a factor in clergy life. There was always a need for instruction of the clergy in theology and languages. But often and in many locations through the Middle Ages, this was little more than an extended catechism. The universities, on the other hand, became magnets for those whose call produced a desire for an intellectually grounded faith. Anselm, Abelard, Aquinas, and others became the formative forces in Christian thought for their eras.

Both because of the secularization of operations as the church became institutionalized and accepted as a legitimate component of national societal structures, and because of the intellectual requirements of a faith understanding, clergy life very early in the history of the church left behind the simple biblical idea of a call of God to a specific ministry. It took on requirements of professionalism similar to those developing in other more secular occupations.

In some ways, the rise of Protestantism interrupted this process and returned the ministry once again to a simpler, more individual and democratically chosen vocation. Much of the impetus of Protestantism was to take the control of the church out of the hands of the hierarchy and return it to the people. As the Scriptures became widely available in the vernacular, anyone might read and discern in them an individual call to ministry.

We have already mentioned how Luther argued that each church should choose its minister from among its spiritually qualified members.

Baptists in America carried this movement to its logical extreme with the farmer-preachers of the frontier. Such men usually had no more than a Bible as their textbook, which sometimes they could not even read. Lacking any kind of regulating hierarchy, all the individual congregation required was that these men feel the call and give evidence of some degree of spiritual maturity. The leap from member to pastor was short both in terms of time and of education.

Of course, most churches did not go that far. Congregationalists, Episcopalians, and Presbyterians all put educational requirements on their clergy fairly early. And the growth of an extensive system of church colleges and seminaries among virtually all denominations had created by the end of the nineteenth century what one might call a normal route for clergy education and certification in America.

To the extent that an individual's call to a specific ministry must be worked out within the context of educational requirements, institutional restrictions, and the natural progression of any career through apprenticeship and experience toward responsibility, ministry has historically built in a gap between the experience of an individual's call and the working out of that call in practical terms. In that sense, Eleanor's situation is by no means unique. It is and in most cases has been the way of the church in the world. The question is "To what degree is this natural gap between experience and execution a biblically and spiritually appropriate reality?"

How does scripture inform an individual's perception and execution of the specific call in ministry?

In our case study, Eleanor perceived her call in terms of preaching and spent her seminary career developing those skills. Then she found herself in a ministry where her primary duties lay in other directions. On the surface, at least, it is hard to reconcile what happened to her with the biblical accounts of calling and service. God called Moses to lead the children of Israel out of Egypt, and lead them he did. God called Jeremiah as a youth to warn Judah of its doom, and doomsay he did. Peter became the apostle to the Jews and Paul the apostle to the Gentiles without much apparent doubt or diversion once they understood their call.

Our long and complex modern process of education, internship, credentialing, and career development seems both mundane and unspiritual by comparison. Part of this is no doubt because it is the high spiritual moments that tend to be recorded and preserved. Yet there is scriptural territory here that has been relatively lightly explored. Without too much risk of eisegesis, one can derive several governing principles for working out one's call in specific terms.

First, scripture suggests a concern for proper credentialing even in the earliest days of the church's self-structuring process. Even if one agrees that the Pastorals were not written by Paul but late in the first century or early in the second century by one of his followers, that still places their concern for ministry qualifications very early in the life of the church. Timothy's list of qualifications for a bishop is classic:

> The saying is sure: whoever aspires to the office of bishop desires a noble task. Now a bishop must be above reproach, married only once, temperate, sensible, respectable, hospitable, an apt teacher, not a drunkard, not violent but gentle, not quarrelsome, and not a lover of money. He must manage his own household well, keeping his children submissive and respectful in every way—for if someone does not know how to manage his own household, how can he take care of God's church? He must not be a recent convert, or he may be puffed up with conceit and fall into the condemnation of the devil. Morevover, he must be well thought of by outsiders, so that he may not fall into disgrace and the snare of the devil. (1 Tim 3:1-7)

Clearly, from the earliest days, not everyone who "felt a call" was admitted to the clergy. A person could be disqualified by character, conduct, reputation, inexperience, and domestic situation. It did not matter what kind of call one felt if that person failed to meet the qualifications required by the church.

We should note, in fairness, that the language of the qualifications for bishop is exclusively masculine. There is no historical evidence of women serving as bishops in the early church. Arguments for placing women in such positions today must be made on the basis of other scriptures. There is, however, a strong argument for the admission of women as deacons that may be made from Timothy's list of qualifications for that office. Using these passages as prooftexts for excluding women from specific ministry positions on the basis of gender should generally be said to be a highly questionable use of the text.

Also note that, using Timothy's requirements, we would never have what we often do in evangelical churches in America today, the spectacle of very recent converts preaching and in some cases leading the church. From the beginning, the church knew that was a bad idea.

Second, scripture suggests a clear criterion of personal suitability for any ministerial task. On one level we might expect, following Peter's vision in Acts chapter 10, that Peter would have become the apostle to the Gentiles. That did not occur. What is more, an objective look at Peter's "blue-collar" Galilean background as opposed to Paul's erudite education and wide experience argues that Paul was certainly better suited to the task.

The idea of personal suitability is further supported by Paul's imagery of the one body with many members:

> Now you are the body of Christ and individually members of it. And God has appointed in the church first apostles, second prophets, third teachers; then deeds of power, then gifts of healing, forms of assistance, forms of leadership, various kinds of tongues. Are all apostles? Are all prophets? Are all teachers? (1 Cor 12:27-29)

Some are called to one kind of ministry, others to another. That suitability is a function not only of background, but also of God-given temperament, interest, and inclination. Part of the problem that arose in the church at Corinth was that some members possessed of the gift of tongues were apparently claiming that their gift made them superior to their brothers and sisters who lacked that gift.

Similar problems arise today, especially in evangelical life, when the gift of preaching is elevated to the exclusion of all others. Some persons who feel a call to the ministry interpret it only as a call to preach without regard to their personal gifts and abilities. Paul's answer, of course, is that each gift has its place and all are vital to the work of the kingdom.

A third applicable biblical principle is the discipline of service. Paul said of his own apostleship: "I have become all things to all people, that I might by all means save some" (1 Cor 9:22). Jew, Greek, slave, free, male, female—the appeal to each situation in life required a particular approach. Obviously, some of these were more comfortable and natural for Paul than others. That the erudite Jew would be comfortable arguing scripture in the synagogue goes without saying. That he learned to sit at table with a Greek jailer and explain the gospel in terms a man he had nothing in common with could understand and appreciate reflects a discipline that Paul must have acquired. It came out of his sense of call to carry the gospel to everyone. Similarly, Paul's willingness to earn his own living by tentmaking instead of using his abilities as a preacher to encourage donations from his followers shows a deep sensitivity to the need to offer the gospel without strings.

From the beginning, Christ connected the idea of leadership within the community of believers to that of service (Mark 10:43-45). We could argue, for example, that the apostles made a misstep in Acts 6 when they appointed the seven to serve tables while they concentrated on the ministry of the word. Suggesting that mundane service is less to be preferred seems somehow out of step with Christ's injunction to find greatness by becoming "the servant of all."

The question of the degree of the apostles' humility aside, however, the appointment of the seven does show the great value placed on service from the inception of the organizational life of the church. That Stephen is reported as "full of faith and of the Holy Spirit" suggests that he, too, might have reasonably expected a somewhat grander leadership role than serving tables. Clearly the church had captured the spirit of Christ's injunction to *diakonos* (minister, servant, deacon). To be Christ's *diakonos* is to do whatever needs to be done, from preaching to serving tables to ministering to the sick to sweeping out the sanctuary. Scripture draws no ultimate distinction with regard to the relative holiness of various tasks within the community of faith.

A fourth principle may be inferred from the difference in scripture itself between the dream and the details. In Acts 9:15-16, after the spirit of Christ had dazzled Saul on the Damascus road, Ananias protested to the Lord. The Spirit answered,

> But the Lord said to him, "Go, for he is an instrument whom I have chosen to bring my name before Gentiles and kings and before the people of Israel; I myself will show him how much he must suffer for the sake of my name."

Later on in his ministerial career, Paul himself cataloged the sufferings his call had cost him:

> Are they ministers of Christ? I am talking like a madman—I am a better one: with far greater labors, far more imprisonments, with countless floggings, and often near death. Five times I have received from the Jews the forty lashes minus one. Three times I was beaten with rods. Once I received a stoning. Three times I was shipwrecked; for a night and a day I was adrift at sea; on frequent journeys, in danger from rivers, danger from bandits, danger from my own people, danger from Gentiles, danger in the sea, danger from false brothers and sisters. (2 Cor 11:23ff.)

The dream that Paul's call gave him did come true. Yet it came true only in and through countless detours and difficulties. His ministry serves as a paradigm for the lot of every one of his successors. There is no biblical reason to expect anything else.

Christ's encounter with Peter in John 21:18ff suggests one final point. Christ had just intimated that Peter would die as a captive. Peter asked, "What about John?" Christ answered, "If it is my will that he remain till I come, what is that to you? Follow me!" Christ never promised that life would be fair or that all his servants would suffer equally in this life. Quite the opposite. He told us that any apparent differences in blessing are none of our business. This is not to say that a social prejudice such as discrimination against women in ministry should be tolerated. It is to say that each person's journey is uniquely his or her own, as each is led by the spirit of Christ. What conclusions, then, can we draw about Eleanor and others who dream of holding forth in crystal cathedrals and find themselves sweeping up sticky construction paper instead?

What are the elements of a theology of specific calling?

The scriptural survey suggests that Eleanor's situation, at least at this point in her career, is not markedly different from that of many men in ministry. Admittedly the element of anti-female prejudice in her denomination complicates our perceptions. There is no reason to doubt that human evil, at least in the short run, can frustrate the purposes of God. If Eleanor's talents continue to be undervalued, most sensible folk would suggest that she find a faith communion more amenable to her ambitions. At the same time, it has been usual and normal through the history of the church for great talents to serve long apprenticeships before they get the opportunity to shine.

Theologically, the call to ministry is preeminently a call to service. By nature, servants do not have the luxury of choosing what they will and will not do. They do what needs to be done, specifically, "I have become all things. . . ." To return to Barnette's aphorism, if we agree that God's specific call to a particular person at a particular time occurs at the intersection of that person's ability and opportunity, then we see that ministry by the very nature of its involvement with specific people in specific situations will encounter countless detours and obstacles.

An able young theologian with a position at Union Theological Seminary in New York, Dietrich Bonhoeffer chose to return to Nazi

Germany, to suffer along with his dear German people, because he believed that is what God wanted him to do. Obviously, as a professional decision, what he did was disastrous. Yet he never doubted he was responding to the clear call of God in his life. I have often known ministers who left secure, prosperous, prominent situations of long standing in order to undertake some perilous new venture. The servants of Christ operate with a unique definition of opportunity.

It is also true that very often, even in this world, what Christ promises about the servant of the least being acknowledged as the greatest takes place. At this writing, unchallenged honors as the greatest woman in the Christian world go to the Carmelite nun Mother Teresa, whose life has been spent easing the dying of the street people of Calcutta.

Is it wrong, then, to enter the ministry from a passionate desire to "become a great preacher" or to "pastor a large church" or to "influence the direction of my denomination?" No, some among us are gifted by God with precisely those abilities and opportunities. Unfortunately, there are a great many in the church who work to create their own opportunities other than through merit. And there are just as many who hold influence who impose criteria other than merit for granting opportunities. We restrict our discussion to the character of the individual minister, however. It is wrong for the minister to allow desire for any status in this world to obscure or replace the desire to serve Christ.

What should Eleanor do? Ultimately, of course, the choice is hers. From our discussion, we have to accept the possibility that the associate ministry in the little church across the tracks remains God's call for Eleanor at this time in her life. Often it is the very frustration with a particular task that makes doing it well a genuine offering of service. Diligent, thoughtful prayer combined with consultation with peers we respect will usually help us clarify whether a particular situation is to be endured or not.

As we have already suggested, if her denomination's structure is hardheartedly contaminated by sexism, many would suggest she find a more congenial communion. Others would ask whether she is called to work for change where she is. Still others might remind her of the personal and psychological dangers of a dream too long deferred. Ultimately, as a child of God, she and all of us must remember that the same God who calls us to service loves us and wants the best for us. That leads us to the next question of this chapter. What are the ethical considerations when a minister wants out of or wants to change jobs within the ministry?

What if I want to get out of the ministry?

Tuesday afternoon was a slow time at First Church, Oak Grove. Senior pastor John sat gazing out his study window toward the playground where the preschool children were coming to the end of another recess. For the thousandth time that year his mind traveled the same circuit.

"How can I go on like this? I'm not happy. Mary isn't happy. I know I'm not doing the kind of job I should, but the truth is I just don't want to be here! No, it's more than that. The truth is I want out of the pastorate altogether. I want to teach history!"

As he idly watched a bank of puffy clouds drifting through the blue skies over the church, John's mind drifted back to his last year of graduate school fifteen years before. He had always been interested in both teaching and preaching and had received good feedback for his ability to do both. Preaching had seemed somehow the easier, more accessible path. After all, churches always needed pastors. Even more, he had felt called. He had seen the need people have for real help in applying the faith to life, and he had wanted very much to be a part of that.

But now here he was in Oak Grove, 500 miles from the nearest denominational college. He was forty-two. Despite his own doubts about his performance, he knew the church was quite happy. But the truth was he disliked much of what a pastor has to do, the meetings with the church board, the pastoral calls on the elderly, the constant invasion of his family's privacy. The truth was he wanted out. He longed for the classroom.

He also found himself in a crisis of faith. Almost the only ministers he knew who had ever left the pastorate were those who had been kicked out for moral reasons, or those who were obviously incompetent, or those who did so well the church called them into the hierarchy. "Is it possible?" he wondered. "Could it be right for me to choose to leave? What happened to my call?"

How has the church dealt with those who wanted to change jobs within or out of the ministry?

Historically a call to the ministry has been viewed as a high and determinative mystical event in a person's life. In Catholicism, the call to a ministerial vocation has generally been seen as a lifelong commitment.

To that end, ordination is generally granted only after persons have demonstrated their vocation (calling) to the satisfaction of their superiors in the church. Once granted, ordination is seen as for life.

A priest, for example, who wishes to leave the clergy in order to marry must obtain special permission to do so within the church. To act without church approval is to guarantee excommunication. By the same token, in Catholic monasticism vows are taken only after an extended period of apprenticeship, and, once taken, are considered binding for life. To live as a "lapsed" priest, monk, or nun—even in the last years of the twentieth century—is to live under a specific ecclesiastical and a somewhat more vague Catholic cultural disapprobation.

Much of Protestant popular culture, similarly, frowns on someone who has "left the ministry." In my own career, at the end of graduate study, I left the pastorate of a small church in Kentucky to work in my denomination's social ethics office. Again and again as I was saying goodbye, the members of that little church lamented the fact that I was "leaving the ministry," despite my best efforts to explain to them that I was following my own sense of God's vocational call. And this was to a job within the fabric of my own denominational structure, one recognized even by the tax authorities as appropriate employment for an ordained individual. Similarly, when I was reentering the pastorate several years later, people congratulated me on "returning to the ministry," despite the fact that my ministry in the denominational office had impacted far more people than a local church pastorate ever could.

Like the Catholic church, most Protestant communions have retained some means of disciplining clergy whose conduct does not conform to accepted standards. The Presbyterian Book of Order prescribes specific procedures for clergy discipline. Several years ago the Assembly of God made national headlines by suspending evangelist Jimmy Swaggart's right to preach for moral reasons. Baptist churches through the years have not infrequently rescinded the ordination of ministers whose actions they disapproved. In the free churches the simplest and most emphatic way of indicating disapproval of someone's ministry is to fire them.

Protestant churches have been less likely, however, than Catholics to impose any formal sanction on the ordained who quit the local church ministry. In fact, I have been unable to locate a single such case.

In Protestant theology the doctrine of the priesthood of the believer calls into question the entire purpose of ordination as a lifelong decision. From Luther onward, Protestant theologians have argued that all believers are called to ministry and that the vocational ministry is simply one aspect of the wider work of the church.

It is a very small step indeed from that argument to an argument for the fluidity of an individual's call allowing movement from secular work to vocational ministry and back again. Henlee Barnette never deals specifically with the justification for a specific minister leaving congregational service today. He does, however, point out that in the earliest Baptist congregations call and ordination were seen as "for a specific task, for a specific length of time; after that function had been fulfilled, the 'ordination' became invalid."[12] It was not till the eighteenth century in Baptist life that ordination came to be viewed as permanent for an individual and valid within all Baptist churches.

Noyce places the issue for mainline Protestantism within the context of personal freedom, citing the case of "Jim" who found freedom on a seminary faculty after years of frustrating confinement within parish ministry.[13] He argues, in effect, that "Jim" simply may not have been psychologically and personally suited to the public demands of the pastorate. There must be a balance, he says, between the public demands of building up a faith community and the personal and private "habits of heart and personal style."[14]

The reasons, then, for choosing to leave the parish ministry could be said to be a mixture of the personal and the professional. Sometimes ministers discover they are not temperamentally suited to a public life. Most ministers in Baptist life, for example, tend to be extroverts. Baptist churches as a whole place great emphasis on "fellowship," visitation of church members, and various types of Christian recreation. Baptist worship tends to be relatively demonstrative. More introverted individuals may find that they simply do not like to do the day-to-day things expected of Baptist ministers. They may find it more difficult than extroverts to carve out a comfortable niche for themselves.

Again in Baptist life in recent years, as in Missouri Synod Lutheran life not long ago, clergy have left the practice of ministry because of theological disputes within the denomination. A close friend of this author recently chose law school over continued vocational service within Baptist life. He simply no longer felt comfortable toeing the theological line of the dominant powers. His own theological convictions had not changed, but the atmosphere within which he worked had changed.

Walter Wiest and Elwyn Smith point out that ministers sometimes leave parish life because their own theological convictions have changed.[15] In those communions that require assent to a particular creed at ordination, a minister may sometimes find he or she is no longer able to support the denomination's faith assertions. Since ministers are normally expected to grow intellectually, such events are hardly surprising.

Not infrequently, ministers choose to leave the ministry because of family problems. Catholic priests may wish to marry. Protestant ministers may wish to divorce. Either choice often means the decision renders the minister professionally unacceptable. Others may find that the time and pressure demands of parish life make it too difficult to spend adequate time with their spouse and children.

This chapter is not intended to deal with forced terminations as such, but rather with the process of making the choice to leave. Nonetheless, it is important to note that forced termination is a problem faced by increasing numbers of ministers. Terminations are forced for moral reasons, as a result of theological disagreements, in recognition of power realities within a congregation, and because of insufficient communication and management skills on the part of both ministers and congregational leadership. For the most part, however, the issue of forced termination is a problem for the congregation and denominational hierarchy to contemplate, rather than an ethical issue for fired ministers.

Ministers who consider leaving the parish ministry today face a set of issues rooted in their personal history, faith journey, and personality. Available biblical guidance is limited to the points of intersection between faith experience in the biblical era and now. Still, we must explore scripture if we are to hope for authentic assistance in this matter.

What biblical teachings inform an individual's decision to leave a ministerial calling?

Perhaps the most obvious biblical reason for leaving a specific ministry is a call to a different ministry. Expositors sometimes forget that Paul's call to Macedonia involved specific calls away from Asia and Bithynia, two perfectly legitimate places of potential ministry (Acts 16:6-10). Nobody ever said Ur of the Chaldees was a bad place. It just was not the place where God wanted Abraham to be (Gen 11:31–12:3). God's call to people of faith often involves a choice between specific alternatives, each of which may in some ways be good.

It is also worth examining the church's first commissioning of Paul and Barnabas in Acts 13. The Spirit directed the church to set the two apart for missions. At the time, Paul was already something of an itinerant minister within the church. The laying on of hands in verse 3 seems to carry little of the cachet of permanence that ordination later gained. Rather, it is the blessing of these two to a particular task at the impetus of the Spirit. As such, there is little reason to suppose that a similar ceremony might not have taken place each time Paul and his companions left their home church for a new task. This argument is somewhat weakened by the fact that toward the end of the New Testament period the writer of Timothy (Paul or one of his imitators) considered the laying on of hands for elders as a matter to be carefully considered over time (1 Tim 5:22).

Obviously the idea of ordination as the church understands it today was only developing in New Testament times. The priesthood in first-century Judaism was hereditary. Certainly there were ceremonies of investiture when one began service in the temple, but priests were born to the task. Prophets might be called from outside the tribe of Levi, but there was no formal sanction for a prophetic career. In the early, more fluid years of the church's structure, it was far more important that a task be accomplished than that the one who did it be formally approved.

The free church concept of the priesthood of the believer (1 Pet 2:9) carries this idea to its logical extreme. Protestants have argued that the ministry is merely one specific function within the larger priesthood of the congregation. All are priests, so, theoretically at least, any should be able to preach, to baptize, to carry out the functions of the ordained. The branches of the Friends church, which lack any clergy, are examples of this idea. Also, by implication, ministers who complete the task to which they were called, or who feel directed toward a secular means of earning a living, are not "leaving the ministry"—because no believer ever does. They are merely altering the origin of their paycheck.

It is interesting to note that within Baptist life today, foreign missionaries are commonly "commissioned" before they leave for the field in a manner not much different from what was done to Paul and Barnabas at Antioch. But they are not considered "ordained." After a term or two, these missionaries often return home and reenter their old occupations or seek out new ones with little or no sense that they have abandoned the ministry. They are simply responding to changing circumstances. There are also a few Baptist churches that have ceased ordaining deacons and ministers altogether, considering the practice unbiblical.

What conclusions may we draw
about the ethics of leaving a ministerial occupation?

Sometimes it is right for a minister to leave the ministry. Sometimes it is wrong. The definitive act for the Christian's life is not his or her call to the vocational ministry but rather his or her call to Christ. I contend that the Protestant understanding of the priesthood of the believer is the definitive biblical image for a concept of Christian ministry. Within that understanding we can posit several situations in which leaving the ministry is an appropriate choice.

When a person enters the vocational ministry, she normally does so at a particular point in her life, with a particular faith understanding, and a fairly specific sense of the task to which she is called. Even someone who simply feels a generalized call to the ministry will most likely have some mental image of what the active content of that ministry will be. Legitimate situations in which to choose to leave the ministry will then flow from changes in the sets of circumstances that prevailed as she made her initial decision.

Sometimes, in the normal process of human growth, a person's understanding of his own capacities and interests will change. John, in our introductory case, had thought in the beginning that the parish ministry was a good vocational choice for him. Experience in the job, combined with the development of his own self-understanding, had convinced him otherwise. Discovering that we do not like what we are doing for a living and wanting to change is such a common human experience that we would never question it with regard to any other vocation. The ministry should not be put under a special burden in this regard, especially if one understands that all believers are priests by virtue of their conversion. Leaving the vocational ministry cannot then by definition be leaving the Christian ministry. No Christian ever leaves the ministry.

It is also sometimes true that family circumstances will change and make a ministerial occupation more problematic than it was at first. We will deal in more detail with the minister's obligations to his or her family in another chapter. Suffice it to say at this point that I will argue the commitment to spouse and family takes priority over how one earns one's living.

A second possibility is that one's faith understanding will change. This is the idea with which Wiest and Smith deal in their section on truth-telling. Obviously, ministers who no longer believe the doctrines of their church are under an obligation of integrity not to continue self-presentation as a believer.

This condition is modified somewhat among non-creedal communions such as the Baptists. Baptists have traditionally placed such emphasis on the conscience of the individual believer that they have allowed considerable latitude for disagreement on points of theology. Holding to a particular eschatology or a particular theory of biblical inspiration, for example, has never been seen as a condition of ministry. Baptist theological latitude, however, has never been unlimited. It has rather allowed primarily for nuances of interpretation within the overall parameters of conservative Christianity. You might expect a Baptist minister to dispute the correct interpretation of the book of Revelation, but you would never expect a Baptist minister to dispute the bodily resurrection of Jesus Christ.

In the free church, ministers whose interpretations no longer accord with those of their church may simply seek a more congenial congregation. In the hierarchical churches, certain inconsistencies may be tolerated within the overall structure of the creed. Ministers who cease to believe substantial portions of dogma, however, should resign as a matter of conscience. The Roman Catholic phenomenon of recent years in which priests have sought to marry and remain priests in good standing illustrates.

Whether the Catholic doctrine of priestly celibacy is right or wrong is immaterial. It is the doctrine, and there is no leeway within Catholic teaching for individual conviction on this matter. A priest who no longer wishes to practice celibacy will usually resign. Inability to staff the churches may finally force the Vatican to reconsider.

A third possible legitimate reason for leaving the vocational ministry is the inability to continue the task to which one was called. That may mean the job is completed. A minister may be called to a particular church for a specific period or passage in that church's history. Continuing in the ministry when that task is completed will depend upon receiving a new call to a different situation or upon reinterpreting one's existing call for the changes where one presently serves.

It may mean the door for ministry is closed in some other way. A number of called and qualified ministers within Southern Baptist life have left the ministry in recent years because of the continued narrowing of acceptable theological parameters for ministers and convention employees. Very often missionaries find that the conditions under which they were called to a particular country or people change, and the service to which they felt called is no longer required. Certainly in this kind of situation, no one would hold a person to a commitment made under different circumstances.

The key concept for the ethics of leaving the vocational ministry is thus the maintenance of personal integrity. Again we come back to the doctrine of the priesthood of the believer. If we accept the idea that every Christian is called to the ministry, whether vocational or not, for as long as they live on this earth, then vocational ministry takes its proper place as one small portion of the larger Christian picture. Movement back and forth between vocational and non-vocational service becomes a function of circumstance, opportunity, and the immediate leadership of the Spirit in the individual Christian life. If John would feel happier and more fulfilled as a teacher, and his desires are confirmed by the counsel of those he trusts and by an objective opportunity, then to teaching he should go.

It remains to deal with the most common "illegitimate" exit from the ministry, that of a moral indiscretion. For all my professional life, common parlance in Baptist circles has held that the most foolproof way for a Baptist minister who wants out of the ministry to accomplish the change is to have an affair or get a divorce. As I have been writing this chapter, no less than two prominent men and one woman near my own age have left the ministry because of extramarital affairs or marital problems.

In Baptist life, exiting the ministry by means of sexual indiscretion has the advantages of being quick, decisive, and usually irreversible. Common psychology has held that this also obviates the necessity of a decision to leave one's calling. The church and community make the decision for the person as soon as the offense becomes common knowledge.

Aside from the obvious moral problem, however, there are at least two ethical difficulties. First, the concept of the priesthood of the believer means that even a fallen priest has obligations. Leaving the vocational ministry in no way releases the Christian from the obligation to serve. Second, while sexual sin may be seen culturally as particularly heinous, it is biblically no worse than any of the more culturally acceptable offenses. There is no more reason, biblically, to remove a person from the ministry for sexual problems, provided those problems do not involve abuse of others or of the power of office, than for greed or gluttony.

We would hope that someone experiencing marital problems or sexual urges incompatible with Christian norms would choose to leave the vocational ministry first, before the damage to family and congregation occurs, rather than change their behavior and allow that change to end their ministerial career. It is not nearly so unchristian to leave a vocational responsibility before ending an unsatisfactory marriage as it is to allow improper behavior both to end a ministerial career and to endanger a marital commitment.

The above observation raises the question of what exactly is Christian and what is unchristian in personal conduct, which leads us in a new direction. The next chapter will deal in more depth with the personal aspect of the minister's spiritual formation, what may best be called the minister's character.

Notes

[1] Tertullian, "Monogamy," in *The Ante-Nicene Fathers*, ed. Alexander Roberts and James Donaldson (Grand Rapids MI: Eerdmans, 1951) 4:69.

[2] Martin Luther, "To the Christian Nobility of the German Nation Regarding the Reform of the Christian Estate," in *Luther's Works*, vol. 44, *The Christian in Society* 1, ed. James Atkinson (Philadelphia: Fortress, 1966) 127.

[3] Ibid., 175.

[4] Gaylord Noyce, *Pastoral Ethics* (Nashville: Abingdon, 1988) 200.

[5] Sydney E. Ahlstrom, *A Religious History of the American People* (New Haven: Yale University Press, 1972) 149.

[6] K. L. Schmidt, "Kaleo," in *Theological Dictionary of the New Testament*, Gerhard Kittel and Gerhard Friedrich, eds. (Grand Rapids MI: Eerdmans, 1985) 395.

[7] Henlee Barnette, *Has God Called You?* (Nashville TN: Broadman, 1969) 18.

[8] Ibid., 128.

[9] Williston Walker, *A History of the Christian Church*, 3rd ed. (New York: Charles Scribner's Sons, 1970) 82-83.

[10] Kenneth Scott Latourette, *A History of Christianity*, vol. 1 (New York: Harper & Row, 1975) 221-22.

[11] Ibid., 524.

[12] Barnette, 118.

[13] Noyce, 184-85.

[14] Ibid., 119.

[15] Walter E. Wiest and Elwyn A. Smith, *Ethics in Ministry: A Guide for the Professional* (Minneapolis: Fortress, 1990) 47.

CHAPTER 2

SPIRITUALITY

Christianity is ultimately a personal faith. How do I, as an individual, live out my own relationship to the risen Christ? For ministers, however, that personal faith has to be worked out in the context of a faith community. Even more, it has to be worked out in public view, as a public example. One need only cite the generally negative example of Jimmy Swaggart or the generally positive one of Billy Graham to call forth dramatic images in most late twentieth-century American minds of what it means to be a public Christian. The pages that follow will set some guidelines for these questions. How do ministers practice their faith in public? How do they practice their faith in private? And what happens when public expectations and private faith conflict?

What are the appropriate
public constraints for my personal activities?

Ed cruised around the block for a second time. There were not many places in his small city where he felt safe entering a liquor store. Teetotaling was the clear public expectation of ministers in Ed's denomination, as it had been since the prohibition crusades of the early twentieth century. Ed, like many of his seminary generation, no longer held that view. In fact, moderate drinking had been a badge of openmindedness before ordination. Ed and his wife Patricia, despite their background, had learned to enjoy wine with dinner on special occasions. It had become one of the few indulgences they could afford.

It had not been so easy, however, once they left the relative anonymity of seminary life and entered the local pastorate. Ed quickly realized that, regardless of what the church leaders did themselves, they expected Ed not to drink and to be opposed to their drinking at least in principle. His first reaction had been amusement, then growing resentment, as he realized a personal freedom he had come to cherish could threaten both his influence and his career.

Quickly he and Patricia learned to restrict their drinking to times when they were out of town or to choose out-of-the-way spots and times to make their purchases and to dispose of the evidence carefully afterward. The more Ed became known in their city, however, the more difficult the clandestine practice became. Now here he was ten miles from home with his heart racing and his palms sweating, all because they had decided they would like a bottle of Burgundy with their steaks on his evening off. Surely that was not deacon Eldridge's car parked in front of the store, was it? What if it were?

What have been the historical expectations for public piety for ministers?

From the earliest days of the church, ministers have been required both to meet certain behavioral criteria for ordination and to live within certain constraints if they wish to remain in the ministry. First Timothy's succinct list is the root from which all such specifications spring:

> Now a bishop must be above reproach, married only once, temperate, sensible, respectable, hospitable, an apt teacher, not a drunkard, not violent but gentle, not quarrelsome, and not a lover of money. He must manage his own household well, keeping his children submissive and respectful in every way—for if someone does not know how to manage his own household, how can he take care of God's church? He must not be a recent convert, or he may be puffed up with conceit and fall into the condemnation of the devil. Moreover he must be well thought of by outsiders, so that he may not fall into disgrace and the snare of the devil. (3:2-7)

One might reasonably think that because the early ministry was a charismatic (in the broadest sense of the term) rather than an institutional ministry, there were few conduct problems in the first generations. Paul's admonition not to feed a prophet for more than two days demonstrates the contrary. Clearly from the beginning there were those who would abuse the goodwill or the credulity of the church.

In an effort to guide the churches in the selection of the best possible candidates, the fathers put forth a number of lists of qualifications appropriate to their particular situations. The Syrian *Didascalia*, quoted in Niebuhr and Williams' excellent summary, suggests the third-century ideal:

> And let him be scant and poor in his food and drink, that he may be able to be watchful in admonishing and correcting those who are undisciplined. And let him not be crafty and extravagant, not luxurious, nor pleasure-loving, nor fond of dainty meats.[1]

One wonders what exactly "dainty meats" were at the time, but apparently too many of them were a bad thing.

For the most part, however, the ministry only began to be an advantageous, and therefore a sought-after, occupation with the adoption of the faith as the established religion of the Empire in the early fourth century. By that time several elements were coming into play that would affect the practice of public piety by ministers for generations.

First there was the adoption of a clerical garb different from that of the laity. To wear a particular kind of robe or to shave the crown of the head in the tonsure made the minister conspicuous as he had not been before. Second, there was the increasing impetus toward clerical celibacy. While this would not be made compulsory till the end of the first millenium, celibacy became the preferred status for clergy in the West quite early. In many ways this standard introduced the first opportunity for an obvious difference between ostensible public commitment and private practice. Third was the increasing sacramentalism of the priestly function. As the priest became more and more a functionary in a mystical rite, that function became divorced in the Christian mind from the piety of the individual priest.

The response to the Donatist heresy is the prime example of this third idea. Augustine himself argued that baptism by a Donatist priest was valid, despite the priest's personal heresy, as long as the priest had been formally ordained in the correct manner.[2] This validity of the sacrament *ex opere operato* meant that, in Catholicism, it was the function of the priest, not his personal character, that came to be seen as necessary to the life of the church.

A fourth change in public expectation was the movement of the church from pacifist indifference to politics to militant defense of the realm of the faithful. With the ascent to power of the church as Rome fell, the priestly life became inextricably intertwined with that of the rulers. The fact that through the Middle Ages the clergy were the only truly educated class drew them even more into secular life and its temptations.

There were, of course, innumerable attempts to reform the public life of the clergy. Not the least of these was monasticism, which attempted to create a place in which a life pleasing to God could be lived apart from the world. Modern folk have a hard time grasping the tremendous influence of the monastics on medieval faith and culture. As was inevitable, the monastics in their turn were drawn into "worldly" corruption. It is also true that many fine, decent, sincere clergy have served in every age of the church.

Having said the above, however, it is still true that Protestantism arose in part as a protest against the failure of the Church to provide a converted clergy. The soul of Protestantism is its reemphasis on the idea of personal conversion to the Christian faith. Luther and those who came after him sought to sweep away the whole vast medieval edifice of Catholicism with its sacramentalism and institutionalism and replace that structure with simple personal response to the Word of God in the person of Jesus Christ.

The concept of the "priesthood of the believer" meant that clergy were no longer so much a class set apart from the congregation as a whole. They were chosen from among the faithful, often by the faithful themselves, depending on the degree of hierarchical organization the particular communion retained. Those who demanded that John Knox enter the ministry did so precisely because they knew everything about his public conduct and believed that his life demonstrated God's call to service.

Standards of public piety for Protestant clergy developed along lines somewhat different from those of the priesthood. In Lutheranism, Luther's own marriage to Katherine von Bora and the family life in their parsonage began a tradition of emphasis on the minister's family life. The English vicarage played something of the same kind of role in Anglicanism. Congregations developed the custom of judging their minister by the appearance of domestic harmony, unity, and fidelity displayed by his family. The eighteenth-century novel, *The Vicar of Wakefield*, and the early nineteenth-century drawing-room novels of Jane Austen give penetrating and often humorous insight into the behavior expected of clergy by the English public.

America's standards of public piety were, of course, colored by the frontier. Baptists, with their lack of a requirement for clergy education, were perhaps most affected. Baptist "farmer preachers" spent their weekdays clearing the land and building cabins and their weekends harvesting souls. Methodist circuit riders might see the congregations they served only once a month or even once a quarter. The early camp meetings of the Great Awakening were high spiritual moments. They were also times for socializing, courting, conducting business, and more than a little drinking. A Kentucky Baptist preacher invented bourbon whiskey as a more efficient means of transporting his and his neighbors' corn to market. It was not till the temperance movement took hold of

Baptist life in the 1830s and 1840s that teetotaling began to become a behavioral requirement for Baptist clergy.[3]

Today, of course, each denomination, according to its own polity, develops and imposes standards for public conduct by its clergy. Most often these standards operate informally, as unspoken criteria for ordination and advancement. Sometimes they are imposed with glaring publicity, as in the Assembly of God's attempts to discipline Jimmy Swaggart for sexual misconduct. Not infrequently, they are invoked by local congregations. Before we decide whether Ed should get in trouble for going to the liquor store, let's see what biblical help we can find in developing an enduring set of standards for public ministerial conduct.

What biblical principles guide us in establishing standards for public ministerial conduct today?

Christianity is a faith of both grace and ideals. Many of its biggest battles have been fought in the struggle to determine to what degree ideals must be met in order for grace to operate. The theological answer, of course, is not at all. Grace is free. But in practical terms, especially with its clergy, the church from the very beginning has held that those who would lead must answer to a higher standard. Jesus himself, despite his overwhelming emphasis upon grace, set the tone for clergy standards in several teachings.

Perhaps most important, he established the standard of servanthood (Matt 20:24-28) about which we will talk much in Chapter 4 as a test for leadership. He inveighed against the false leadership of the scribes and Pharisees,

> But woe to you Pharisees! For you tithe mint and rue and herbs of all kinds, and neglect justice and the love of God; it is these things you ought to have practiced without neglecting the others. . . . Woe also to you lawyers! For you load people with burdens hard to bear, and you yourselves do not lift a finger to ease them. Woe to you! For you build the tombs of the prophets whom your ancestors killed. (Luke 11: 42, 46-47)

Clearly Jesus was creating the highest standards of public conduct for all his followers, and especially for those who would be leaders of others.

It was left to the church, however, to codify standards for pastoral and other leadership. The Timothy passage quoted in the beginning of this chapter provides nothing less than the basic minimum of public conduct for ministers. Several points are worth noting.

First, the bishop (pastor) must be "above reproach." Such a leader's conduct must be such that no one has cause to reprove him or her. Obviously, specific aspects of this standard have varied somewhat from time to time and from culture to culture. American Baptists would at one time quite happily accept a pastor who smoked tobacco but immediately dismiss one who drank beer. German Baptists of the same period would think nothing of a pastor drinking beer, but fire one who smoked tobacco. The key is that conduct must be suitable to the time, place, and congregation served.

A second phrase, translated "married only once" in the NRSV, has caused, quite literally, no end of trouble to interpreters and churches alike. Does it mean married only once within a lifetime, never divorced, or not a polygamist? In some denominations a minister's divorce is grounds for instant dismissal. In others it is a cause for prayerful, concerned support. My own sense of the passage in context is that the author means "not a polygamist," precisely because polygamy was such a common part of first-century life. Still I know no serious Christian leader who would view divorce and remarriage as less than cautionary in evaluating a minister's leadership potential.

The second marital standard, "managing his own household well," is of course far more widely ignored and abused than the former one. And yet nothing undermines a church's respect for their minister more quickly than for the minister to have a bad marriage or an undisciplined child.

The personal public front the minister displays must be moderate and controlled. Moreover, it must be more than a newly assumed lifestyle. The individual must have been Christian long enough for Christian ways and values to have permeated his or her personality. With regard to alcohol, specifically, the passage does not require ministerial abstinence, but it does require temperance. Baptist tradition particularly has taken this stricture in combination with Paul's injunction "not to cause the weaker ones to stumble" in 1 Corinthians and developed in America a strict expectation of ministerial teetotaling.

The extension of that controlled lifestyle requirement to money shows that the church was aware from the very beginning of the potential for financial abuse of congregations by their pastors. One has only to cite dramatic examples such as the Jim Bakker fraud trial in the

United States to see how vital this particular standard of ministerial conduct remains.

The final public requirement for ministerial conduct listed in the letter to Timothy is to be "well thought of by outsiders." The phrase is interesting and would bear much examination. Exactly how do the clergy gain a good reputation among the secular opinionmakers of their neighborhood?

It is perhaps best considered, however, in tandem with Paul's teaching concerning the effect of eating food that had been offered to idols on members of the church with tender consciences. Paul argued,

> Since some have become so accustomed to idols until now, they still think of the food they eat as food offered to an idol; and their conscience, being weak, is defiled. Food will not bring us close to God. We are no worse off if we do not eat, and no better off if we do. But take care that this liberty of yours does not somehow become a stumbling block to the weak. For if others see you, who possess knowledge, eating in the temple of an idol, might they not, since their conscience is weak, be encouraged to the point of eating food sacrificed to idols? So by your knowledge those weak believers for whom Christ died are destroyed. But when you thus sin against members of your family, and wound their conscience when it is weak, you sin against Christ. Therefore, if food is a cause of their falling, I will never eat meat, so that I may not cause one of them to fall. (1 Cor 8:7b-13)

This particular teaching of Paul's comes in the context of a much longer treatment of the balance between personal liberty and obligation to the church. On balance, though, Paul's point seems to be that Christians, and therefore especially Christian leaders, must curb the expression of their own freedom in Christ where that expression might harm the spiritual life of those in the church who are less mature. Clearly something of the same exemplary behavior must characterize the Christian leader's relationships with those outside the church. We are back to the "above reproach" idea with which the Timothy passage begins.

The writer of Titus adds a further word concerning the bishop's theological soundness:

> He must have a firm grasp of the word that is trustworthy in accordance with the teaching, so that he may be able both to preach with sound doctrine and to refute those who contradict it. (1:9)

Today, no less than in the early church, a minister's job is in part to defend the central teachings of the faith against adulteration or misinterpretation. The Bishop of Durham's (England) rather callous annual insistence on debunking popular conceptions of the Christmas story, and thereby confounding the faithful and delighting the infidel as a byproduct of demonstrating his own scholarly prowess, is one good contemporary example of how the minister's public piety ought not be expressed.

How should ministers govern personal public conduct in the light of their status as ministers of Christ?

Walter Wiest deals with this problem in an excellent chapter titled "The Pastor as Human Being."[4] He observes,

> Totally to subordinate person to profession reduces the self to a caricature. . . . On the other hand, for the minister of the Word, it is wrong to deny the subjection of self in fundamental ways to the demands of the calling (as distinct from "job" narrowly considered). Psychological health requires that life be integrated. Theologically speaking, those who cannot tolerate the demands of the calling must reconsider the genuineness of their call. There is no reproach in this. We make mistakes in religious matters as in all others.[5]

Wiest cites Lebacqz's discussion of the need for a "role morality" for the minister and for a limit to how far one will allow the demands of a role to impinge upon the authentic self.

The key here is for ministers as much as is humanly possible with divine assistance, to match the job and the job context they accept to their own convictions regarding the living of the Christian life. Ed's problem is that the religious culture he chose for himself in seminary did not match the religious expectations of the parish culture within which he found himself working. He is ethically wrong in attempting to keep a foot in both worlds. His choice becomes the choice between acceding, or giving in, to the requirements of his job situation and finding another more congenial context in which to work.

In this sense, scriptural guidance and modern professional and psychological standards are in agreement. The first requirement for ministerial leadership is that the individual hold the convictions of the community freely and firmly. This does not mean, at least in the free churches, that the minister's personal theology and ethics must agree at every point with the convictions of the community he or she serves. There is room for personal disagreement. Indeed the minister would have little to teach her parishoners if she agreed with them about every matter of faith and practice beforehand. It does mean that the minister must be prepared to live out his convictions in a manner that the community as a whole will consider acceptable and even exemplary. Ed is in the position of having accepted an obligation to lead without being willing to do so in fact. It doesn't matter ethically whether he manages to evade detection. What matters is the incongruity between ostensible conviction and actual behavior.

The first principle of public piety for ministers is thus that of being "above reproach" within the context in which they choose to minister. Note that this contextual piety is very real. My wife and I, ourselves usually abstainers and part of a generally teetotaling denomination, were once interviewed by representatives of one of our "country club" churches. The interviewers said at one point, "We're just looking for someone who can come out to the club with us after the university football games and sit around drinking Bloody Marys." We confessed our usual preference for Diet Coke and were promptly eliminated from consideration for that pulpit.

A second principle of public piety relates specifically to business and financial dealings. A minister's personal finances, credit dealings, and business practices must always be in good order. This is increasingly difficult in a society driven by credit, but it is nonetheless essential.

A third principle of public piety relates to the requirements mentioned in both the letters to Timothy and Titus regarding the minister's self-control. Timothy suggests that the minister be "temperate, sensible, respectable, hospitable . . . not violent but gentle, not quarrelsome" (3:3). Titus puts it as "a lover of goodness, prudent, upright, devout, and self-controlled" (1:8). The church has a right to expect that the minister's behavior in every situation will be appropriate to the demands of the moment. A pastor who loses his temper in a business or committee meeting or a minister of music who stomps out of a choir rehearsal in a fury can undo in a few moments years of careful, patient nurturing of a relationship with a congregation. By the same token, a minister who is known in her neighborhood for off-color exclamations or contentious relationships with the neighbors has effectively blotted her public image and that of her church.

A fourth principle of public ministerial piety relates to the whole matter of family. We will deal in more detail with the minister's relationships with his or her family later. Suffice it to say at this point that the minister will inevitably be judged by the congregation on the basis of family relationships. An out-of-control child, a difficult marriage, a divorce, a questionable dating relationship—any of these and a thousand other details of the minister's family life will be regarded by the church as more or less public property.

While all of this can be enormously frustrating, the minister's obligation is not to have a perfect family, but to work consistently toward developing a healthy family life as any Christian would. To the extent that the minister succeeds and his or her family becomes an example to the church of good Christian family life, so much the better. On the other hand, admitting to the church that one's family is not perfect can be an enormous encouragement and an effective teaching tool as church members struggle to deal with their own flawed families.

The minister's family life becomes an impediment to continued effective ministry when there is serious moral failure or when the stresses of dealing with a marriage or a child become such that job energy and performance are seriously and lastingly impaired. Family members who refuse to conform to the congregation's expectations of the ministerial family may also place the minister in the position of having to choose between job and family. If Ed's wife not only insisted on a private glass of Burgundy but also insisted on serving it when the deacon officers of that teetotaling congregation came to dinner, Ed might find his private dilemma escalating quickly and alarmingly.

One further observation remains to be made regarding the public piety of the minister in the realm of family life. In terms of ministers I have known, no single ethical issue has been responsible for more people losing their ministry than personal relational or sexual misconduct. The problem is so common that my seminary generation joked that ministers who wanted out of the profession but lacked the courage to make the decision on their own would accomplish their wish by having an affair and letting the church make the decision for them.

I have not dealt systematically with the ethical problem of ministerial sexual conduct because I see little room for discussion. He must be a faithful husband. She must be a faithful wife. A single minister must be celibate.[6] Ministers should eschew pornography and may indulge in erotica only to the degree that such enhances the marital relationship. None of this restricts full and free sexual expression within a marriage. Nor do I intend to suggest that a minister should remain trapped for the sake of ministry in a loveless or irretrievably broken marriage. I simply say that the decision to break a marriage vow other than in the most carefully considered divorce or to become sexually active as a single minister usually is and probably should be a decision to leave the ministry. The principle of a life lived above reproach and the inevitable judgment of a minister in terms of his or her family life necessarily limit ministerial sexual ethics to the highest possible standards.

What are the appropriate private standards for the expression of my faith convictions?

The late Grady Nutt told the story of the way his personal piety changed after he entered seminary. Before seminary, he and his wife Eleanor would often end their day reading their Bible together in bed. After he had been in seminary a few months, there came an evening when Eleanor wanted to follow their former custom. Grady said he took the book and threw it across the room shouting, "I read that damn Bible every day of the week at school. The last thing I want to do is read it at home with you!"

I don't remember exactly how Nutt said he and Eleanor worked out their dilemma. Their problem, however, is typical of the personal/ professional stresses experienced by many in ministry today. Most people enter the ministry from a profound sense of personal conviction and calling. Many of them are distressed in the extreme to discover that in many ways the ministry is a profession like any other.

Just as the medical doctor assumes a certain professional aura when she walks into her office, the minister takes on the cachet of the profession when she is in public. That ministerial persona must be maintained regardless of how pious or faithful the minister happens to feel on a given day. The inevitable result is a pressure toward a division over time between the minister's own personal convictions and his professional stance as that is maintained for public consumption. At the same time, observers of contemporary religious life report a growing hunger, especially among the Baby Boomer and Baby Buster generations, for ministers with a deep sense of personal spirituality who are able to pass that spiritual experience along to their congregants.[7]

What are the historical roots of personal ministerial spirituality?

Because Christianity is a deeply personal religion, its ministry from the beginning has been made up of those who experienced a deep sense of personal calling. From the day when Christ walked by the seashore and called Peter and Andrew to "fish for people," individuals' imaginations have been fired and their lives and careers changed by the desire to build Christ's church. From the week when Judas went to the high priest and accepted thirty pieces of silver and Peter's courage failed in the high priest's courtyard, that ministerial commitment has been subject to abuse and betrayal by those who make it.

It is of course impossible to quantify any answer to a question such as "How many ministers of the gospel through the ages have also been sincere, practicing Christians in their private life?" Such records are kept only in divine precincts, wherein this writer as yet lacks a reader's permit. It is possible to suggest that the problem of a gap between professional status and personal spirituality likely did not become significant until the ministry began to assume the status of a profession with the Constantinian establishment.

To take the fourth-century church as an example, by this time the different orders of clergy—bishop, priest, and presbyter—were becoming fairly clearly defined. The ministry was becoming a profession. In addition, there were numerous minor clerical posts that might be seen as stepping stones to greater responsibility. The monastic movement was already in its infancy, protesting the growing worldliness of the church as a whole.

Yet the dominant view of the pastoral office of bishop was very high indeed. George H. Williams commented that many of the best hearts and minds of the era were reluctant to become bishops precisely because they viewed it as a post of great spiritual responsibility and great spiritual danger. He cited four reasons. (1) They preferred to devote their energy to "Christian philosophy" or monasticism as a means of working out their own salvation. (2) With Chrysostom, they believed a true pastor must be ready to perish for the sake of his congregation. (3) They dreaded the stricter judgment awaiting those who assumed great responsibility. (4) There was a "holy fear that bordered on awesome dread" surrounding officiating at the Eucharist.[8]

This extremely high view of the ministry that dominated the age was somewhat countered in its effect on subsequent eras by Augustine's development of the idea of the validity of correct ministerial actions regardless of the character of the priest. In Augustine's understandable coping with the Donatist heresy we see the seeds of the great abuses of ministerial office that characterized certain periods of medieval

Catholicism. If the sacraments can be valid regardless of who administers them, then any rogue can be a priest.

With Christendom's domination of Europe, the church's servants of course became prey to all the power struggles and corruptive potential of politics. Many sincere Christians opted for monasticism rather than the priesthood as by far the safer route to heaven. Neither path was immune to the spirit of the age. Priests and monks alike became first business people and then soldiers as the church took over the commercial and military functions of medieval Europe.[9]

In answer to this businesslike reality there began to develop, especially in the cloister but also in some quarters of the church itself, a strong emphasis on personal spirituality. John of the Cross, Teresa of Avila, Saint Francis of Assisi, and many others within medieval Catholicism followed a path of mystical communion with the divine and sought to communicate their vision through writing and preaching to the church at large. In many ways they were the spiritual ancestors of the Protestant emphasis on individual piety, though their Catholic souls would recoil at the very thought.

With the Reformation came a new emphasis on personal piety, the salvation of the individual not through loyalty to the church but through direct communion with the divine, an emphasis that was to find expression again and again in the life of the church down to our own day. Many of the Reformation churches attempted to return New Testament era standards of personal piety. The Puritan movement in England was designed to accomplish much the same kind of reform in the Anglican church. Protestantism, however, proved no more immune to secularizing influences on the clergy than medieval Catholicism had been.

As a result, clergy in the modern era have always lived in tension between the secularizing demands of day-to-day church and community life and a call to an intense personal and devotional spirituality. The eighteenth-century English cleric William Law exemplified this in his *A Serious Call to a Devout and Holy Life*. For Law, the common round of English parish life failed to be serious in its attempt to follow Christ. Similarly, it was a personal spiritual experience which set afire the tinder of John Wesley's arid soul and led to the movement called Methodism. The Great Awakenings in America were awakenings of clergy as much as of people. Nineteenth-century revivalism sought to keep alive the fires of devotion by regular intense preaching on conversion and personal holiness.

The tension in the American church has often taken the form of an apparent war between intellectualism and piety. Baptists, particularly, have demonstrated a history of suspicion of an educated clergy. People in the churches were afraid that "too much" education would destroy their ministers' enthusiasm for winning souls for Christ. In some ways the whole fundamentalism/modernism debate that has characterized the twentieth century in America could be said to result from the fear that ministers who learned too much of the world would lose their devotion to Christ and lead their congregations away from the path of true salvation. Southern Baptists have graphically demonstrated that fear in the 1980s and 1990s by dismantling the faculties of their two most academically oriented seminaries and requiring that all six institutions impose biblically literalist standards for faculty.

The question is what it has always been. In the light of the managerial/entrepreneurial demands of parish life, under the constant criticism of academic theology and popular culture, and given the human qualities of their own emotional/spiritual condition, how do ministers maintain an authentic personal spiritual life?

What scriptural principles apply to the personal spiritual life of ministers?

We have already dealt with the ethical aspects of a call to the ministry, so we will not repeat them at this point. Suffice it to say that the minimum biblical requirements for ministry are that the minister be converted, that is, a convinced personal follower of Jesus Christ; and called, either by spiritual intervention or by spiritual inclination, to serve.

Jesus is of course our primary model both for ministry and personal spirituality. Luke emphasizes Jesus' own need to isolate himself for prayer at regular intervals and especially at significant moments in his ministry. His formal ministry began with the retreat to the wilderness (Luke 4: 1-14) where he clarified his own sense of God's leadership. Just before choosing the twelve (6:12), he spent a night on the mountain alone in prayer. In 9:18, he examines the progress of his ministry while alone with the disciples in prayer. In 9:28, he takes Peter, James, and John up on the mountain with him to pray. While our popular piety imagines that Jesus enjoyed an uninterupted pipeline to God's presence, scripture shows that he disciplined himself to regular intervals of retreat and prayer.

A second aspect of personal spirituality is found in Jesus' emphasis on the role the Holy Spirit would play in the life of the disciples (John 14:16-17). As comforter, as advocate, as teacher of truth, as guide, as companion, as source of power, the Spirit is available to all Christians. In ministry, the New Testament speaks again and again of the role of the Spirit in directing and empowering the believers. The coming of the Spirit in Acts 2 ignites the ministry of the church in the first place. In Acts 7:55, Stephen is filled with the strength of the Holy Spirit at the moment of his persecution. In Acts 16:6, Luke speaks matter of factly of the Spirit's guidance in the matter of where to preach the gospel next. Ministers must seek the constant indwelling companionship of the Holy Spirit in every aspect of their public and private life.

Third, scripture requires the minister to adopt a personal attitude and practice of servanthood. Matthew 20:24-28 is the key passage. Simply put, no minister may use the ministry to gain personal power or prestige. The minister is to be characterized by a personal spiritual attitude of servanthood.

Paul's instructions to Timothy and Titus regarding bishops, deacons, and elders list a range of qualifications that amount to maturity in Christ. Somewhat more personal is Paul's caution to Timothy to "let no one despise your youth, but set the believers an example in speech and conduct, in love, in faith, in purity" (1 Tim 4:12). Paul also encouraged Timothy to work diligently at his own understanding of the Scriptures: "Do your best to present yourself to God as one approved by him, a worker who has no need to be ashamed, rightly explaining the word of truth" (2 Tim 2:15); and to "continue in what you have learned and firmly believed, knowing from whom you learned it" (3:14).

The summary idea would seem to be that the minister must first be a sincere, competent practitioner of the faith in order to be able to lead the church or pass that faith along to others. In the earliest days of the developmental process toward the professional ministry, the minister's personal spirituality was simply to be that of a convinced, mature believer. Paul did give Timothy practical advice toward managing the different groups that would make up the church, but nothing in that advice was intended to suggest any divergence of Timothy's personal faith from his necessary practice as leader of the church.

What standards apply to the
development of the minister's personal spirituality today?

In many ways this discussion of the minister's personal spirituality amounts to an attempt to deal with what many who have written about ministerial ethics in recent years have called the minister's character. Character in this sense amounts to the qualities of the minister's individual spiritual personality. Lebacqz suggests that ministers share many of these characteristics with other professionals and emphasizes that we are not concerned so much with a list of dos and don'ts as we are with the qualities of a person's nature.[10] Wiest argues the profoundly human and fallible nature of professional ministry even at its best:

> Indeed there is something wryly anomalous about ordained sinners seeking to become accomplished prophets, teachers, and priests. The figure of the Pharisee warns us: the person who knows how to pray expertly is the Pharisee. Only if there is something of the hopelessly unprofessional publican within can one hope for authenticity in the clergy life.
>
> Any human being immersed every day in the practice of a profession continuously experiences the impact of professional demands upon the self. The mature professional is a person who has grown through this process without sacrificing individuality and personal integrity.
>
> An authentic professional ethic is simply the system of behavior freely adopted by a called person. That behavior in turn expresses a view of life rooted in deeply felt convictions.[11]

That ministers frequently fail is simply a demonstration of humanity rather than of lack of suitability for the ministry. The first aspect of an ethics of spirituality for ministers is therefore that they, before all else, are recipients of grace. Ministerial character is formed in receiving that grace and passing it along to others.

In this sense, the spiritual life of ministers is identical with that of all other believers, especially in the free church traditions that emphasize the priesthood of the believer. As they practice the spiritual disciplines, ministers gain the depth of personal spiritual maturity that informs and gives substance to Christian experience. Richard Foster's *Celebration of Discipline* was written for the average Christian rather than specifically for ministers.[12] At the same time, the disciplines Foster suggests—study, prayer, service, simplicity, and so on—serve as a kind of laundry list of characteristics for the kind of spiritual depth expected of ministers.

Prayer, solitude, and time for spiritual reflection are especially important in the development of the minister's spirituality given both biblical teaching and the increasingly noisy, busy nature of contemporary life. Neither Wiest nor Lebacqz finds room to deal with prayer as an important aspect of ministerial character and practice. Perhaps they assumed that ministers would be people of prayer. Yet, both from the example of Jesus and the experience of the apostolic age, prayer is an essential ethical aspect of the practice of ministry. Prayer returns the minister to spiritual home base, provides the touch with the eternal that guards ministerial actions from too much subjectivity, and taps into the source of power that is the motive force of Christian life. The minister who does not pray has nothing to offer the world.

A minister should therefore cultivate a personal devotional life that makes time for regular daily prayer. That prayer life will then undergird the moment-by-moment walk with the Holy Spirit, which the monk Brother Lawrence termed "the practice of the presence of God." In my own dissertation I showed how the Baptist ethicist Henlee Barnette regarded this leadership of the Holy Spirit as an essential element of the process of ethical decision-making.[13]

Ministers should then combine the discipline of prayer with regular study both of the Scriptures and of Christian devotional texts (study is another of Foster's spiritual disciplines) as well as of theology and current sociological and other scientific information. This study will provide the objective input in the light of which a Christian life is lived.

We should say, with relation to the Nutts' dilemma with which we began this section, that there is a difference between the devotional study one might expect to characterize an individual's or couple's daily Bible readings and the rigor of academic inquiry into the Scriptures. A passage one has analyzed in depth in its original Greek in the morning may nonetheless offer devotional insights in the vernacular when read at family devotions in the evening. Indeed, that difference points to perhaps the crux of what needs to be said about the ethics of a minister's personal spirituality. A professional Christian is nonetheless a personal Christian first. No one should become a minister who is not first a believer, and every believer requires personal practice of his or her faith, ministers no less than laity.

Having attended Nutt's seminary myself not long after he did, I can attest that its life in that period majored on academic inquiry as over against personal devotion. But that was exactly what it was intended to do. It did not exist to teach ministers how to be good Christians, but rather to prepare practicing Christians for the professional ministry.

The purpose of the minister's spiritual discipline is not to make the individual a better minister but to help the minister become a better Christian. In fact, this very spirituality may on occasion lead the individual away from the practice of professional ministry rather than toward it. One of my personal heroes in ministry once told me that he reviews his own place in ministry at least every few months. He regularly asks himself questions such as "Am I using my talents to the fullest for God's glory?" and "Could I serve better in some other context?" More than once that process has led him to change his place of service. The final section of this chapter will help us look in some depth at issues surrounding a conflict between a minister's personal convictions and the context in which he or she presently serves.

What should I do when my faith convictions conflict with those of my faith community?

In 1979, at its annual convention in Houston, Texas, the Southern Baptist Convention witnessed the beginning of an organized, systematic, political campaign by fundamentalists to take over the power structure of the convention and thereby to control the direction of its institutions. The mechanism for achieving control was quite simple. All the fundamentalists had to do was to control the election of the convention president for a period of approximately ten years. The president controls the appointment of trustees to all the governing boards of the convention's agencies. The trustees determine the agencies' policies.

Trumpeting an extremely narrow definition of biblical inerrancy in combination with a right-wing political agenda, the fundamentalists won. By the late 1980s, they had achieved political control of the entire national structure of the convention, its executive board, its publishing house, its social ethics agency, its seminaries, and its home and foreign mission agencies.

Policies that the convention's left wing (known as moderates) considered anathema began to be enacted across the board. The entire left wing of the denomination, amounting to approximately forty percent of the convention by most estimates, found its people and its opinions unrepresented in the convention's policies and power structure. Once firmly in power, the leaders of the takeover declared that the controversy was over, called on the losers to continue their contributions to the convention's national work, and began to say that everyone should reconcile on the basis of the new power reality.

Baptist polity, of course, with its strong emphasis on the priesthood of the believer and the autonomy of the local church, gave a good deal of room for dissenting ministers and congregations to continue to hold to their own practices and biblical interpretations. But, from a moderate perspective, the well of national convention life was poisoned. The question we will attempt to answer through this section is "How could or should dissenting ministers act when their faith community adopts a stance they find contrary to their personal convictions?"

How have dissenting ministers historically related to the majority in Christian life?

Christian history is of course replete with examples of clergy who have opposed their own opinions to those of the majority in the church. In the earliest centuries it was precisely through the give and take of theological controversy that the contours of Christian orthodoxy were sketched. From Arius who taught that the Son was not a part of the Father through Nestorius who wished not to call Mary the "mother of God" to the Donatists who contended that the validity of baptism and ordination depended on the character of the one officiating, the early church was a sea of controversy.

In answer to these controversies came the councils of bishops who met to determine the correct or orthodox teaching. The Bishop of Rome became increasingly influential and, in the latter half of the first millenium, took his place as the preeminent authority in the church hierarchy. More and more the Church attempted to impose its authority on the sundry opinions of various dissenters, but it was never completely successful in doing so.

The views of the British monk Pelagius in the early fifth century are as good an example as any of the kind of controversy that was common. Pelagius held that each person at birth is capable of choosing the good. No less a figure than Augustine countered with his articulation of the doctrine of original sin. Pelagius' views were condemned by the Council of Carthage in 419, and the bishop Zosimus issued a letter condemning the monk along with his views. Pelagius disappeared from history at this point, probably dead by 420. His views continued to cause trouble however. They were condemned again by the Council of Ephesus in 431. Still they have reappeared in one form or another to the present.

As Catholicism gained sway, dissenters sometimes found themselves to be starting a rival church, whether they particularly wanted to or not. In 1176, Peter Waldo, a rich merchant of Lyons, decided to take literally Jesus' injunction to the rich young ruler to "sell what you have and give to the poor." He became a preacher of the simple life. As such, he quickly gathered a significant following of humbler folk, who came to be known as the "Poor Men of Lyons." They acted as traveling preachers, seeking to conform to the New Testament, teaching that the papacy was corrupt, that prayer could be efficacious outside the churches, that sacraments administered by corrupt priests were invalid, and that women and laymen could preach.

The Waldenses were excommunicated by the Pope in 1184. Still they persisted, providing their own clergy and settling in the Italian Alps. They became in effect a periodically persecuted church within the Church. Remnants of their fellowship united with the Swiss Reformed churches 400 years later at the time of the Reformation.

The Reformation was a time of much courage. The perhaps apocryphal declaration by the monk Martin Luther to the Diet of Worms— "Here I stand, God being my helper I can do no other!"— is one clear example of an individual taking a stand of conscience in the face of majority opposition. The courage of the Anabaptists, whom Luther himself wished to baptize permanently, is another.

In England, Thomas Cranmer played a major role in the reformation of the Church of England instigated by Henry VIII's marital adventures. Cranmer himself was a devout man of good character. With the rise of Mary to the throne at Edward VI's death, Catholicism was restored. Cranmer at first went along with Mary, then refused, and he was burned at the stake in a pubic square in Oxford. It is said that at the stake he held the hand with which he had signed the recantation Mary demanded in the fire so that it might be the first part of his body reduced to ashes.[14]

No clergy of the Reformation faced such consistent and universal condemnation by both civil and ecclesiastical authorities as the radical reformers of the left. Because the Baptists and Quakers abandoned the traditional forms of worship and took their authority from the Scriptures and the Holy Spirit rather than from the hierarchy of the favored church, they were hated and feared by virtually every establishment in both Europe and America. American history is rife with the lore of briefly Baptist Roger Williams and his founding of Rhode Island as the first colony with freedom of religion. Baptists have long claimed that it was their John Leland who cut the deal with James Madison that led to the First Amendment to the United States Constitution.

The American spirit, particularly, has lent itself to the multiplication of denominations by theological controversy. In the absence of any controlling theological establishment, preachers who disagreed could simply go over into the next valley or down the river a few miles and start a group of those who agreed with their new interpretation. Many preachers did just that. William Miller's Adventists, Joseph Smith's Mormons, and Mary Baker Eddy's Christian Scientists are all excellent examples of this purely American phenomenon.

The primary question we're asking in this section, however, logically precedes any such break as the founding of a new denomination. The question is: How do ministers act when they find themselves in direct conflict with the dominant teaching of their own communion?

Baptist life in America offers several examples of such events. In the 1890s, Dr. W. H. Whitsitt, who was at the time president and professor at the Southern Baptist Theological Seminary, published a book called *A Question in Baptist History.* The purpose of the book was to answer the claims of the popular Landmark movement in Baptist life. The Landmarkers claimed, among other things, that Baptists could trace their lineage through an unbroken succession of groups holding Baptist principles stretching all the way back to the founding of the church at the time of the resurrection.

Whitsitt answered this highly dubious claim with careful scholarship arguing that the beginning of Baptists came with the "recovery" of baptism by immersion in England in 1641. He was soon attacked in a storm of controversy. Successionism had a firm hold on the popular Baptist imagination, and nothing so puny as scholarship was about to weaken that hold. Several Baptist state conventions passed resolutions asking for his forced retirement. The controversy grew more and more bitter. Finally B. H. Carroll, a leader of Texas Baptists, gave notice that at the 1899 Southern Baptist Convention he would seek to withdraw all Southern Baptist ties and financial support from the seminary. Whitsitt resigned. He left the politically sensitive world of the denominational seminary and became a professor at the Virginia Baptist institution, the University of Richmond.[15]

Nearly seventy years later, the Midwestern Baptist Seminary professor Ralph H. Elliot found himself involved in a similar brouhaha. Elliot had written a book on the message of Genesis which was published by the Southern Baptist Convention publishing house, Broadman Press.

He argued that the first eleven chapters of Genesis, were largely symbolic rather than historical fact. His views were roundly condemned by the 1962 Southern Baptist Convention. The Board of Trustees of Midwestern thereupon asked him to agree not to republish his book. Elliot refused and was fired for insubordination. He thereupon left Southern Baptist life and became a part of the more theologically open American Baptist Convention.[16]

Baptists are not the only denomination subject to such struggles of conscience in the late twentieth century. In the 1980s, the Missouri Synod Lutheran school Concordia Seminary split over issues of biblical interpretation. Literally hundreds of Catholic priests and nuns left the clergy in the 1960s and 1970s rather than continue to observe the prohibition against clergy marriage. Roman Catholic theology professors both in Europe and America have not infrequently found themselves in conflict with their superiors over a range of teachings. The Episcopal Diocese of Fort Worth remains at loggerheads with the national church over its refusal to accept the ordination of women to the priesthood. One neighborhood Episcopal parish priest led his congregation out of the Anglican communion entirely and into Western rite orthodoxy as a protest against what he regarded as the liberalism of the national church.

Clearly the question of how a minister proceeds when in conflict with the teachings of the church crosses all lines. It beats in the very heart of Christian conviction.

How does scripture illuminate the issue of individual versus community conscience?

In one sense, all of scripture is the story of men and women of faith acting on their convictions regardless of the odds or the opposition. Abram left Ur of the Chaldees at the call of God to start the history of the Hebrew people. Moses defied the gods of Egypt to bring the Children of Israel out of captivity. The prophet Hosea ridiculed and rejected the religious establishment of the northern kingdom when he found them to be unfaithful to the God of Abraham, Isaac, and Jacob. Esther saved the Jews from the politico/religious wrath of Nebuchadnezzar.

Certainly a major theme of Jesus' ministry was his opposition to the stultified and rigid religion of the Jewish establishment. He called others to just such an approach:

> Blessed are you when people hate you, and when they exclude you, revile you, and defame you on account of the Son of Man. Rejoice in that day and leap for joy, for surely your reward is great in heaven; for that is what their ancestors did to the prophets. (Luke 6:22-23)

Jesus thus positioned himself in the tradition of the prophetic challenge to the establishment, urged his followers to take upon themselves a similar kind of challenge, and promised them a reward in heaven and their own place in the prophetic tradition for so doing. With this kind of basic background there is little wonder that Christians through the ages have taken up opposition gladly when their convictions have been at stake.

In fact, many commentators argue that it was the direct challenge to the religious establishment of Judaism that led to Jesus' crucifixion. John's Gospel sets the cleansing of the temple early in Jesus' ministry as a public act of defiance of the status quo. The other Gospels place the event in the week of the Passion, but all of them show it to be a signal act that aroused the chief priests, scribes, and elders to seek a way to destroy Jesus.

Jesus also saw himself as shepherd and as in that sense responsible for the well-being of his sheep. His final injunction to Peter in John 21 is the charge to take on the shepherd role, to "feed my sheep." Indeed the very word "pastor" is a transliteration of the word for shepherd. The minister thus has a responsibility to guard the flock and to keep them from harm. No true minister can fail to act when the spiritual or physical well-being of the sheep is at stake.

Did Jesus really expect his followers to act as he did? After all, he understood himself to be unique, the Messiah. Did he actually intend his disciples to imitate his active, confrontational approach to the religious establishment? Apparently he did. At the very least, the book of Acts and the stories of Paul's journeys indicate that the early church as a whole acted on its convictions regardless of fear or favor.

A particularly telling example within the church is the dispute that arose at Antioch regarding table fellowship of Jewish with Gentile believers. Peter, resident in Antioch at the time, had been accustomed to eating with Gentile believers as a matter of course. Judaizing elements from Jerusalem arrived and were severely critical of this departure from Jewish law. Peter at first drew back, conscious of their criticism. But Paul argued successfully that Peter had thus violated his own convictions regarding Christian freedom.

Note the dynamic. Peter was well on his way to becoming the most influential of the Apostles. At the very least he carried great influence as a favorite companion of Jesus. Paul, with his disgraceful background, was something of an upstart in the faith. Yet Paul did not hesitate to oppose Peter "to his face" (Gal 2:11-14) over a matter of ethical practice. He pointed unhesitatingly to the ideal of Christian freedom.

In Galatians, of course, Paul is talking primarily about freedom from the strictures of observing the Jewish law. Here, nonetheless, we find one of the seedbeds for the growth of the Christian idea of freedom of conscience. Whenever any particular culture or religious establishment or power structure has sought to narrow the bounds of Christian practice, Christians have returned again and again to these arguments to find support. Martin Luther's tract on "The Freedom of a Christian Man" recaptures Paul's basic idea for Protestantism. The "free" churches of the radical Reformation extend this idea into the very structure of their organizational life. The old African-American spiritual captures the feeling of Paul's defiance, "And before I'd be a slave, I'd be buried in my grave and go home to my Lord and be free."

Paul's ostensible instructions to Timothy point us toward a positive view of the minister's task in the face of opposition. At Ephesus, there were those who had wandered away into "different doctrines" (1 Tim 1:3). Timothy's job was to keep to the central doctrines of the faith, to teach them and insist that they be followed regardless of any pressures.

> Whoever teaches otherwise and does not agree with the sound words of our Lord Jesus Christ [i.e., as Paul interprets him!] and the teaching that is in accordance with godliness, is conceited, understanding nothing, and has a morbid craving for controversy and for disputes about words. (6:3-4)

Again in 2 Timothy, Paul urges that the young preacher "be persistent whether the time is favorable or unfavorable; convince, rebuke and encourage, with the utmost patience in teaching" (4:2-3). The minister's job is to know the central teachings of the faith and defend those with integrity against all challenges. It is this dogged, persistent, consistent faithfulness in spite of opposition that Paul believed would win for himself and for those who imitated him, a "crown of glory."

One can hardly conclude a survey of scriptural teachings regarding integrity without at least a brief reference to The Revelation to John. We lack the space for a thorough exposition of the various interpretations of Revelation. This author adopts the view that Revelation is primarily to be seen in the genre of apocalyptic literature, highly symbolic language intended for a late first- or early second-century audience that would have been familiar with the form and understood how to interpret it for their own day. The gist of the book may then be seen as an encouragement to Christians to remain faithful in the face of persecution. That theme, the importance of maintaining one's convictions at all costs, forms a major, fundamental motif in Christian teaching.

What ethical guidance can we derive for Christian ministers in conflict with the dominant convictions of their communion?

We return now to the question with which we began this section: "How could or should dissenting ministers act when their faith communion adopts a stand contrary to their faith convictions?" The answer one gives depends on several variables.

First, what is the specific ecclesiological\theological context within which we are operating? Traditionally, the hierarchical churches, especially Catholics, have placed a much greater emphasis on the necessity for obedience than have the free churches. Because Catholics believe that the Church is the conduit for grace, it is a very serious matter indeed for a Catholic to put himself or herself into conflict with the hierarchy of the church. Such a decision might, quite literally, be seen as affecting one's salvation.

Quakers, at the other end of the spectrum, admit to no authority beyond the Holy Spirit's inspiration of the individual conscience. Most churches center their faith and practice on some working document such as the Presbyterian Book of Order. Baptists historically have been reluctant to impose any creedal requirements on either clergy or laity. The "Baptist Faith and Message" statement of Southern Baptists arose out of theological controversy and was intended to state what most Baptists believe about central matters of the faith. The introduction to the 1963 version of that document, however, explicitly affirms the traditional Baptist doctrine of "the soul's competency"[17] and argues that each Baptist is free to interpret scripture.

It would seem therefore to be a much less serious matter for a Baptist to oppose her convention's stance on an issue than for a Catholic to reject the church's teaching. Certainly as affecting salvation it is.

A second variable, however, is the nature of the disagreement. Few American Catholics hesitate to practice contraception, regardless of the church's teachings against it. Catholics generally regard the number and timing of their children as a private matter over which the Church has no right to exercise control. On the other hand, despite widespread opposition, Catholics generally acquiesce in the Church's demand that clergy be celibate. What happens in the rectory is seen as much more directly the concern of the Church than is what happens in the bedrooms of the parish laity.

Large sectors of Baptist laypeople continue to regard the controversy that has torn the Southern Baptist Convention since 1979 as a "preacher's fight," essentially irrelevant to their own life and ministry in the local church. They believe that the same thing will happen this time as happened in the past. After a while things will quiet down, and the convention will get on with its central work of sharing the gospel. For them, the current controversy is just one in a long series of disputes basically irrelevant to the convention's central task.

A third variable thus arises: the intensity with which one holds to a dissenting opinion, the degree of centrality that opinion occupies in one's conception of the faith. Within the Southern Baptist Convention controversy two primary issues exemplify the dilemma that dissenting ministers face.

There is the issue of the nature of biblical authority. Fundamentalists have imposed a definition of biblical inerrancy that requires new employees of boards and agencies to affirm the historicity of the first eleven chapters of Genesis, the literal existence of Adam and Eve, and the authorship of all biblical books by those named as authors in the text. Until recently, such doctrines had not been taught in the convention's seminaries for forty years. Their affirmation requires the virtual rejection of all modern scholarly techniques.

A second issue is the question of the ordination of women as deacons and ministers. Until recently, Baptist polity regarded the question of who should be ordained as a local church matter. While Southern Baptists had not ordained a woman pastor till 1964, there had long been churches in some regions that practiced the ordination of women to the diaconate. Since the advent of fundamentalist control, however, the convention has explicity, in a nonbinding resolution, disapproved of the ordination of women. Moreover, the Home Mission Board has refused to provide funding for churches that call women as pastors. Seminary presidents have been elected who, while providing theological education for women, explicitly disapprove their service as pastors.

Neither of these two issues would be considered central to salvation by moderate Baptists. Yet the intensity with which dissenting opinions are held on questions such as these has become a primary issue of integrity. Many seminary professors and other convention employees now hold opinions explicitly contrary to those of the controlling faction. Do these people go on working for those whose convictions they deplore? What about ministers who find themselves in the position of asking congregations to support financially the ministries of agencies whose policies they find theologically and/or morally abhorrent?

The Scriptures seem to require that the individual act with integrity any time either a fundamental doctrine or an ethical derivative of that doctrine is at stake. For Paul writing to the Galatians, the issue of salvation by grace rather than by adherence to the law was a fundamental doctrine. The question of whether Greeks needed to be circumcised to enter the church was a derivative practice that brought the doctrine into focus within a specific context.

There is no biblical evidence that belief in the literal inerrancy of the Scriptures as present-day Southern Baptist fundamentalists are interpreting that belief is required for salvation. Salvation does, however, require repentance, an authentic turn away from error and toward the truth. For a Baptist minister who does not believe in that definition of inerrancy to appear to support it in order to retain a job or avoid controversy would appear to violate the standard of integrity derived from one's basic commitment to Christ.

Similarly, the biblical evidence is inconclusive regarding whether women should or should not be ordained for service as ministers and deacons. First-century culture argued against it. The purifying fire of the Spirit appears in certain instances at least to have broken through those cultural prohibitions. But, for a Baptist who believes that equality of all persons before Christ is a basic tenet of faith, aquiescing in the barring of women from ordination is unthinkable. Women's equality in Christ today can be no less important an issue than was the equality in Christ of slaves before the Civil War.

What conclusions can we draw? First, ministers are ethically bound to oppose even majority opinions within their own communion when they believe them to be improper expressions of central tenets of the faith. This is true regardless of the relative emphasis the particular communion places on obedience to church policy. Indeed to fail to speak out on matters of conscience is to fail to follow the model that Christ himself set forth for his followers.

Second, when opposition within the context of the communion is no longer possible, a minister may be ethically bound to seek a more congenial forum for expression of his or her beliefs. Many Catholic priests who chose to marry in recent years have entered the Episcopal church. Southern Baptists have always believed in the value, indeed the necessity, of the minority voice. Yet the current fundamentalist creed-alism governing the convention leaves little or no room for vocal opposition within the organization itself.

A professor who teaches techniques of biblical criticism is in danger of censure or dismissal. A pastor who ordains women as deacons or encourages women to enter the ministry may be blacklisted in terms of any convention post of responsibility. Baptist clergy who believe strongly that biblical literalism and/or the oppression of women are wrong seem to be left with little room for maneuver. Either they abandon their conscience, or they abandon their commitment to freedom of expression in Christ, or they abandon their loyalty to the SBC.

Is it not possible, though, to disagree quietly and hope for better days? It is certainly possible politically. Indeed that is perhaps the course most clergy of all denominations would choose when confronted with such dilemmas of conscience. Yet I can find no persuasive support either in scripture or in history for adopting such a course of action. To do so is to worship other gods than the God of truth. In the context of Christian commitment, private, unspoken dissent is not possible ethically.

Moreover, as shepherds of others, ministers must be committed to ethical leadership. To fail to lead on matters of faith and practice is to abdicate the role of shepherd given to us by Jesus. The only course of action for a true servant of Christ in times of conflict is to do what must be done for the sake of the integrity of Christian witness and accept whatever consequences there may be. In the next chapter we will examine how ministers work out their witness in the toughest arena of all, the realm of family life.

Notes

[1] *Didascalia Apostolorum,* ii 5, R. Hugh Connolly, trans. (Oxford: Clarendon Press, 1929) 34; quoted in H. Richard Niebuhr and Daniel Day Williams, eds., *The Ministry in Historical Perspective* (San Francisco: Harper & Row, 1983 revision) 54.

[2] Ibid., 74.

[3] Baptists have always displayed a marvelous inconsistency on this point. As a seminarian I served a small two-century-old congregation on the edge of the Kentucky Bluegrass. It fascinated me that the congregation fully expected me to preach against smoking, drinking, and gambling while they continued quite

happily to make their livings raising tobacco, working in the local distilleries, and raising race horses!

[4]Walter E. Wiest and Elwyn A. Smith, *Ethics in Ministry: A Guide for the Professional* (Minneapolis: Fortress, 1990) 97-120.

[5]Ibid., 102.

[6]The question of homosexual ordination and therefore of the sexual expression of homosexual ministers is becoming more common. At this writing, the German Lutheran church has approved ordaining practicing homosexuals. The Episcopal church is debating the matter. The 1993 Southern Baptist Convention moved toward changing its constitution to explicitly disfellowship any church that approved of homosexuality. I have chosen to place extensive discussion of this issue beyond the scope of this book and to deal in terms of the normative church. Nonetheless it should be said that the expected behavior standards for all ministers are to be those explicitly set forth within their communion. If a denomination, according to its own polity, explicitly determines that homosexuals in committed relationships or homosexuals who remain chaste may serve in its ministry, then individual ministers within that communion are ethically bound to follow that standard. Homosexuals who wish to practice their sexual preference and serve as ministers in a denomination that forbids such practice must either change their vocation or alter their sexual practice.

[7]"Seminaries Renewing Focus on Spirituality, Profs Say," *Baptists Today,* January 1994, 9.

[8]George H. Williams, "The Ministry in the Later Patristic Period (314–451)" in *The Ministry in Historical Perspective*, H. Richard Niebuhr and Daniel D. Williams, eds. (Harper & Row: San Francisco, 1983) 68-69.

[9]Roland H. Bainton, "The Ministry in the Middle Ages," in *The Ministry in Historical Perspective*, 82-85.

[10]Karen Lebacqz, *Professional Ethics* (Nashville TN: Abingdon 1985) 63-106.

[11]Wiest and Smith, 181.

[12]Richard J. Foster, *Celebration of Discipline: The Path to Spiritual Growth* (New York: HarperCollins, 1988).

[13]Ronald D. Sisk, "The Ethics of Henlee Barnette: A Study in Method" (unpublished Ph.D. diss., Southern Baptist Theological Seminary, 1982).

[14]Kenneth Scott Latourette, *A History of Christianity, Volume II, Reformation to the Present* (New York: Harper & Row, 1975) 801-809.

[15]Walter B. Shurden, *Not a Silent People* (Macon GA: Smyth & Helwys, 1995) 9-17.

[16]Ibid., 69-81.

[17]Herschel Hobbs, *The Baptist Faith and Message* (Nashville TN: Convention Press, 1971) 4.

CHAPTER 3
STEWARDSHIP

The Old English term is "sty ward," keeper of the pig sty. From that humble, rather smelly beginning comes our term stewardship. Yet the derivation is more apt than one might suppose. The aspects of ministerial ethics we address in this chapter tend to be messy, neglected, some would say self-absorbed. We look at the everyday life of the minister. How does a pastor take adequate care of his family? How many hours are too many for a minister of education to spend at the church? How does a youth pastor take good care of herself as God's child? What is the distinction between ministry as a calling and as a job? How do you know when to consider yourself a messenger from God and when an employee of the church? We look at the minister's family life, personal well-being, and use of time.

How do I balance family life and ministry?

It was 8:30 Friday evening. Brenda finally sighed, got up from the table, blew out the candles, and picked up the platter of brisket for one last warm-up trip to the oven. Mike had promised faithfully that the early evening emergency meeting of the education committee would not go past 7:00.

"It's Friday, Honey!" he had soothed in answer to her protest. "Everybody else wants to get home as badly as I do! We'll have a good dinner and still make it to the second feature."

Brenda had heard that kind of promise before. When she married a minister of education she had known some of his work would have to be done evenings and weekends when church members were free from their jobs. But she had never dreamed he would be out five nights a week virtually every week of the year.

Now she was expecting their first child, and she found herself wondering if this was how it would be always. Would she be raising their child alone?

They had talked about Mike's schedule before—argued really. Usually sooner or later he took refuge in God talk. "But, Honey, I thought we agreed this is what God wants us to do! Are you asking me to neglect the church?"

Till now Brenda had retired from the field confused when Mike appealed to the Lord's will. Was she just being selfish? Was his schedule the cross God had for her to bear? Somehow tonight, though, those arguments just weren't good enough any more. She'd felt the baby kick this afternoon, and all her self-preservation instincts had kicked into high gear. Was Mike going to be a husband and father, or wasn't he? It was time they found out.

She heard the car door slam and quick, apologetic steps come toward her through the kitchen. Chin up, she turned for the battle.

How have ministers historically dealt with their obligations to their families?

This issue is of necessity relatively new in church history. By the fifth century, Roman Catholicism had dealt sweepingly and effectively with any concerns related to ministerial families by imposing the discipline of clerical celibacy. For the next milennium a priest's family life in the Western Church, if he had any, was treated under the category of sin.

It was not till Martin Luther married Katherine Von Bora on June 13, 1525 that the minister's family life again became a factor that must be managed for those who would serve the Lord. Soon, of course, virtually all Protestant ministers were married. Indeed the Protestants rather quickly began to look with suspicion upon ministers who were not. As Pauck observed,

> The married ministry came to demonstrate that family life . . . can be a more effective vehicle of religion and the service of God than asceticism, celibacy, and otherworldliness.[1]

Luther and Von Bora had six children, three of whom lived to adulthood. The lively family life of their parsonage quickly became a center and a model for the congregation. Katherine demonstrated a strong will and a fine mind, entertaining not only Luther's followers but also nonconformists whose convictions she admired.

Similarly in England, the Reformation raised again the possibility of clergy marriage. Henry VIII was opposed to the idea, and when he appointed Thomas Cranmer Archbishop of Canterbury, Cranmer was required to keep his wife as a mistress until after Henry's death. Edward VI passed the Act of Convocation in 1649, which allowed clergy marriage, but his half-sister Mary revoked the privilege, and even the great Protestant Elizabeth I appears to have had a hard time accepting the institution.[2] The story is told that on ending a visit to the home of Archbishop Parker, Elizabeth took leave of his wife with the words: "Madam I may not call you, Mistress I will not call you, but yet I thank you."[3]

Still by the next century the institution was well established. In 1652, George Herbert wrote *The Country Parson* as a description of the ideal of English parish life:

> The Parson is very exact in the governing of his house, making it a copy and model for his Parish. He knows the temper, and pulse of every person in his house, and accordingly either meets with their vices, or advanceth their virtues. His wife is either religious, or night and day he is winning her to it. Instead of the qualities of the world, he requires only three of her; first a training up of her children and maids in the fear of God, with prayers and catechizing and all religious duties. Secondly, a curing and healing of all wounds and sores with her own hands; which skill either she brought with her, or he takes care she shall learn it of some religious neighbor. Thirdly, a providing for her family in such sort, as that neiher they want a competent sustenation nor her husband be brought in debt. His children he first makes Christians and then Commonwealth's men. . . . in visiting other sick children, and tending their wounds, and sending his charity by them to the poor, and sometimes giving them a little money to do it of themselves. . . . He afterwards turns his care to fit all their dispositions with some calling, not sparing the eldest but giving him the prerogative of his Father's profession. . . . However he resolves with himself never to omit any present good deed of charity, in consideration of providing a stock for his children; but assures himself, that money thus lent to God,is placed surer for his children's advantage, than if it were given to the Chamber of London.[4]

Herbert thus set a Puritan tone for English parish life with an idealized paternalistic image of what the ministerial family ought to be.

Across centuries and cultures Herbert's ideas of the ministerial family have remained remarkably accurate. Jane Austen's nineteenth-century portraits of English life are not inconsistent with Herbert's conceptions at all. In the 1940s an American evangelical pastor's wife, Dorothy Harrison Pentecost, wrote of *The Pastor's Wife and the Church.* The book was intended to be an encouragement to young women who were married to ministers. Its chapter on "Problems of the Pastor's Wife" amounts, however, to a telling indictment of the American ethic of the ministerial family. The minister's wife "has a full-time job in the church's work, even though the public does not realize it."

> One disillusioned and weeping parson's wife said, "No minister's wife is supposed to have children, especially sick ones. She is supposed to have no housework, no ideas of her own, she must never be tired, never want a vacation or want any time to herself."

There is "the heartache she experiences because she is usually placed second in her husband's life."[5] While Pentecost acknowledged that these problems arise mainly from unfair expectations, the gist of her argument seems to be that the mature minister's wife, with the Lord's help, will simply learn to cope with such expectations rather than attempting to change them.

Lucille Lavender's classic 1986 book *They Cry, Too!* gives us perhaps the best-humored summary of the church's skewed expectations:

> A minister's wife should be attractive, but not too attractive; have nice clothes, but not too nice; have a nice basic hairdo, but not too nice; be friendly, but not too friendly, be agressive and greet everyone, especially visitors, but not too aggressive; intelligent, but not too intelligent; educated, but not too educated; down-to-earth, but not too much so; capable, but not too capable; charming, but not too charming.[6]

That these expectations are skewed did not begin to become a significant strain of opinion until the rise of feminism and the marriage enrichment movement. With these two cultural developments, clergy marriages began to come under serious scrutiny.

Statistical and analytical studies such as *What's Happening to Clergy Marriages* have gone a long way toward bringing understanding of the pastoral family into a new era.[7] At the head of a list of nineteen disadvantages of clergy marriage cited by ministerial couples were (1) the church's expectations that the pastoral marriage be a model of perfection, (2) the time pressures created by the minister's schedule, (3) the lack of family privacy, (4) the lack of adequate pay, and (5) the isolation created by a lack of opportunities for friendships in the church.[8] Significantly, the demands and expectations placed on clergy families seem to have changed relatively little since George Herbert wrote so long ago. What has changed is our understanding of the ethics of how the clergy family should order its life in the parish. We begin with an examination of the biblical witness.

How does scripture inform
an ethic for the minister's family relationships?

At first glance, traditional interpretations of scriptural teachings on marriage and ministry militate against much change in our view of a minister's relationship with his/her family. Indeed, the pictures of a minister's family life we have seen are simply somewhat idealized examples of a traditional Christian understanding of family life in general.

There is no question that the Bible is a primarily patriarchal book, written in and for a culture that assumed male dominance in the church, the home, and society. Nor is there any question that traditional interpretations of the biblical idea of calling have emphasized the primacy of the call to ministry over all domestic claims and ties. Jesus himself is the primary authority cited:

> For I have come to set a man against his father, and a daughter against her mother, and a daughter-in-law against her mother-in-law; and one's foes will be members of one's own household. Whoever loves father or mother more than me is not worthy of me; and whoever loves son or daughter more than me is not worthy of me; and whoever does not take up the cross and follow me is not worthy of me. Those who find their life will lose it, and those who lose their life for my sake will find it. (Matt 10:35-39).

There is no evidence that Jesus was talking about anything equivalent to a modern call to the vocational ministry. More likely, he was talking about the faith commitment of Christians as a whole. Yet (even in those churches that deny that women should serve as ministers), the passage has often been interpreted as though it applied directly to a ministerial call. In a ministerial context the teaching is taken to mean that family must never be allowed to come between the minister and his work. Women were taught that it was an honor to be married to a minister and that they must accept their husbands' frequent absences and distraction as their own particular cross to bear. In the interest of being "worthy" of Jesus many a ministerial family has endured a home life not worthy of the name.

The question is "Must we accept this traditional reading as the normative biblical insight on ministerial families?" If so, a progressive ethic of ministerial family life would necessarily find a post-biblical basis, a situation with which evangelicals usually find themselves very uncomfortable.

My own answer is that a substantial biblical basis for a healthy ministerial family life can be found. The first point from a Baptist perspective would of course be that of the priesthood of the believer. Since Baptists believe that all Christians are equally called to ministry and that the vocational expression of that calling is no holier than any other Christian's vocation, a consistent Baptist family ethic would argue that the minister's family should be burdened no more than any other family in the church. To look for the minister's family obligations, we look for those of every believer.

In Ephesians 5 and 6, Paul makes a determined effort to Christianize the first-century family within the context of its normative first-century structure. He does not directly challenge the dominance of the husband and father, but he places the father under obligations that will necessarily alter the family structure itself. The tone is set in 5:21. In a world in which the husband effectively owns the wife, husband and wife are now to "be subject to one another out of reverence for Christ." That mutual submission adds to the domestic contract and the sexual bond an obligation of caring that transforms the entire relationship.

No longer can the man simply use his wife to run his house and produce his children. Her feelings, her wants, her needs become a legitimate concern in Christian marriage in a way in which they have never been before. The effect of Paul's teaching is not to perpetuate a patriarchal pattern but rather to begin the spiritual work of transforming an entire cultural way of thinking and acting. That his words have often, even usually, been taken as establishing a male hierarchy as the Christian pattern of marriage is both ludicrous and tragic.[9]

In the same way, the father, who in the Graeco-Roman world owned his child to the point of the power of life and death over them, is charged in 6:4 to bring them up gently enough not to "provoke your children to anger." Yet virtually anyone who has spent much time in church life can recall tales of minister's child after minister's child who grew up furious with the church because, in effect, he or she either had a father full of rigid expectations or had an absentee father, more married to the church than to his own family.

Timothy, of course, requires that the minister

> must manage his own household well, keeping his children submissive and respectful in every way—for if someone does not know how to manage his own household, how can he take care of God's church? (1 Tim 3:4-5)

Ephesians, however, is the prior, and more generally acknowledged as authentically Pauline, teaching. A reasonable interpretation would be that "managing his own household well" would mean that the minister should bring up children gently and lovingly, not provoking them to anger but eliciting from them the obedience that comes from a heart that experiences and understands submissive love. In effect, then, the spirit of the teaching should not be seen as one of harshness and rigidity, but rather as authentically Christlike.

The context of the teaching should also be remembered. The writer of Timothy was talking about the spiritual and emotional maturity that must be brought to the management of the church. Which of us would want a pastor who was harsh, rigid, neglectful and demanding? How odd that generations of Christians should have thought something of the kind was expected of Christian fathers who were ministers!

One further biblical principle should be suggested. In the first creation account in Genesis 1, male and female are created for one another before either of them is given anything to do (vv. 26-27). Then they together are given dominion over the earth and charged to "fill the earth and subdue it." In this account, then, family comes before vocation. Husband and wife are charged equally with the work to which God calls them, both the work of home and of garden. Division and domination in the human family are presented not as aspects of creation but rather as consequences of the Fall (see especially Gen 3:16).

Some, of course, would argue that this perspective on scripture is more a result of post-1960s feminism than of authentic biblical interpretation. No one is suggesting that the Bible is predominantly other than what it is, the story of a patriarchal people's struggle to understand and respond to the God of creation. Yet the significant fact to this author is that, even in the midst of such a patriarchal structure, one can find threads of teaching that suggest strongly that the impulse of the Spirit is toward authentic caring partnership in the Christian family rather than toward structures of exploitation and domination.

What ethical standards can we derive for ministerial family relationships in the 1990s and beyond?

In the twentieth century the issues related to ministerial family life have grown more complex with the society and the ministry. As this chapter has been written, the German Lutheran church has legitimated the ordination of gay pastors within their communion at almost the same time that an American Lutheran congregation is defying canon law to support its own openly gay pastor. Also during the writing of this chapter, the Church of England has ordained its first women priests, a group of thirty-two. The fact of mothers as pastors and the increasing frequency of dual-ministry families make it even more difficult to construct any kind of meaningful ethic for Christian ministerial families. Nonetheless we shall try.

The first principle, it seems to me, is that, after the Christian's relationship to God, family comes first. It is important to get this right. The tradition in the church has been that once called of God to ministry, ministers were at least tacitly expected to put the ministry before their families. One must draw a clear distinction between the Christian's primary obligation to Christ and any Christian's obligation to his or her job. Most of us would have no trouble at all with the idea that an executive's family should come before her job with AT&T. Yet if that executive is a Christian, our theology of the priesthood of the believer tells us she has the same basic call to ministry as if she were a pastor.

We must realize that ministers are simply Christians who make their living in a particular way. Their relative obligation to family and job is the same as that of any other Christian. In order to teach a congregation that family is the most important human relationship, ministers must make and keep their own families their most important relationship. That primacy must be in fact as well as in theory. We will deal in the next section of this chapter with the specific issue of ministerial time.

Another way of saying this is to say ministerial families have a *prima facie* right to first consideration in the establishment of ministerial priorities. The family bond is the primary social structure of human life. Certainly it comes long before the church.

A second principle is that ministerial families may not be expected to sacrifice for the church to any greater degree than the average Christian family might find it necessary to sacrifice for the husband or wife's career. Traditionally in Protestant life the minister's wife and children weren't allowed to indulge in the same pastimes and amusements as the rest of the congregation. As Mace said,

> There was to be no work done on Sunday, no intoxicating liquor, no motion pictures, theater, or professional entertainment, no dancing or tobacco, no card games, no singing of "secular" songs or reading of "secular" books.[10]

Even now ministers' families are expected to be demonstrably more "holy" than those of the congregation. The idea was supposedly to set an example of Christian family life. More often, for most communities, it amounted to simple hypocrisy.

We must remember that often the minister's spouse and always the minister's children do not choose a public lifestyle. Indeed, based on our analysis of both Genesis 1 and Ephesians 5, regardless of how strong a call one feels, if his or her spouse is opposed to a life in the career ministry, the commitment to spouse takes priority. Under God, the minister "wannabe" must make a living some other way. I have never yet seen a case in which a minister actually left the ministry because his or her children would be better off in private life, but I have seen any number of cases in which the minister should have done so.

A third principle, implied but not specific in what we have already said, is that career ministers must learn to make a clear distinction between their call to serve Christ and any specific job in ministry. A call is a metaphysical reality that colors one's perspective on all the rest of life. A job has a job description, a salary, a supervisory structure, and a specific set of social and performance expectations. You can't quit a call without affecting your relationship with the one calling. You can quit a job. You can renegotiate a job description.

All of this brings us back to Mike and Brenda. More power to her. I hope he listens. Otherwise a family, a church, and the kingdom may be in for damage that need not take place. To help in any similar negotiations, we turn in the next sections of this chapter to the matter of the minister's stewardship of his or her own personal well-being.

How do I care for my own personal physical and emotional well-being?

The regular Monday meeting of the Tarrant County Baptist Association pastors convened around the table at noon just as usual. For many pastors, this was the one meeting of the week when they could more or less relax and be themselves. Brad was glad to be here. As a young pastor in his first full-time parish, he found himself looking forward to the things he could learn from these old hands. The fellowship was warm. The meal was Tex-Mex. Most everybody seemed to be a lifetime member of the clean plate club.

As the program began to drone by, Brad took another sip of his third cup of coffee, unobtrusively loosened his belt a notch, and began to look around the room at his colleagues. "It was scary!" he told Sue that night after supper. "There wasn't a person there over forty who wasn't overweight! I started counting those I knew of who had had heart surgery or ulcers or diabetes. I really started to wonder if there's something about the ministry that's bad for your health!"

Sue sat down and put her practical good sense to work. "Just look at the schedules you keep!" she pointed out. "I'd bet the only exercise most of those people get is a round of golf from a cart. Then there are the church dinners. And almost everyone you visit tries to feed you something."

"So what do I do?" he countered. "I can't be rude to people. It's a social profession."

"Maybe so, but isn't gluttony on that list of deadly sins Paul gives? We Baptists would fire a pastor in a moment for adultery, but we'll listen to a 300-pound slob pontificate and call him a man of God! It's time we thought about keeping you in decent shape!" She began looking at him with a speculative eye.

Brad padded off to the den with a funny feeling he had started something. To make himself feel better, he stopped by the refrigerator to grab a piece of fudge on the way.

What historical support is there for the minister's care of his/her personal well-being?

Of all the historical sections in this book, it is perhaps most difficult to find significant material for these sections regarding ministerial self-care. There are several reasons why this is so. To begin with, a religion whose founder spoke of the necessity of taking up one's cross is hardly likely to spend a great deal of time focusing on such matters as proper nutrition, sleep, and exercise. Christianity began in conversation with Greek and Roman cultures that were, if anything, too much focused on the body.

Secondly, the dominant strain of Catholic faith early adopted a body-denying asceticism as its mystical ideal. A faith that lionized Simeon Stylites for spending thirty years living on top of a pillar and John of the Cross for kneeling in broken pottery was hardly likely to pay much attention to the parish priest's state of physical fitness.

Finally, concern about the minister's health is perhaps a sign that the age itself is less focused on mere survival than in earlier times. The Baptist farmer preachers of the American frontier most likely did not have to deal with the weight problem their sedentary great-grand-children in ministry face today. Nor was physical fitness such an issue for those who lived much closer to death at the best of times than we do today.

From the earliest days of the church, a certain asceticism was the ideal for the clergy. George Williams quotes the *Didascalia*, the Syrian canon law, as requiring the bishop to "be scant and poor in his food and drink, that he may be able to be watchful in admonishing and correcting those who are undisciplined."[11] The point of the asceticism was not so much the physical well-being of the minister as it was the minister's moral influence. A thousand years later in Calvin's Geneva, ministers were subject to weekly meetings for mutual counsel. Such offenses as drunkenness, greed, and so on were regarded as "irreconcilable with the ministry."[12] But again these concerns were not raised for the welfare of the ministers themselves.

Similarly, the Lutheran Visitations uncovered many instances of improper behavior by ministers,

> The most common complaint about them was that they drank too much. It was frequently reported that preachers spent their time sitting around in taverns and that many of them had the habit of staying at wedding parties until the last keg of beer was consumed.

The suggested remedy was radical:

> In 1541, the Hessian Superintendents sent the following petition to the Landgrave Philip: "In view of the fact that there are current many complaints about parsons who scandalize people by their excessive drinking and other disgraceful vices and yet remain unpunished as well as unreformed, we suggest that the jail at the cloister of Spisskoppel be restored and that the parsons who persist in their vices be given the choice either to leave their parishes or to be confined in this jail for a period of time the length of which shall depend on the nature of their offence, in order that on water and bread they may undergo corrective punishment."[13]

The bread and water were of course intended as a moral more than a physical corrective, though they may in some cases have had a salutary physical effect as well.

By the time of George Herbert's *Country Parson*, we begin to see the outlines of the modern "heroic" ideal of ministerial endurance. Every day was to be filled with preaching, catechizing, visiting, consolation, study, and hospitality, from early in the morning till late at night.[14] Winthrop Hudson observed,

> What is astonishing is that there were many who exceeded the rigorous routine he [Herbert] prescribed, who added a weekday lecture to

the Sunday schedule of sermon and catechizing, or who, like Richard Greenham, "rose each morning at four, and spoke to his people at dawn every weekday morning."[15]

We shall deal with Greenham in the section of this chapter on the minister's time commitments. The point here is that from its beginnings the modern concept of the ministry shares much with the ancient in its high and demanding expectations of ministerial endurance.

It was not till the nineteenth century that the reforming spirit began to require changes in ministerial behavior for reasons of stewardship as opposed to morals. At the beginning of that century, Baptist ministers were still hearty participants in the drinking that went on as a matter of course in frontier life. By the 1840s, the temperance movement had begun to make serious inroads in the frontier's alcohol-tolerant culture. The New Hampshire Confession of 1855 specifically forbade alcohol to committed Baptists.

Contemporary interest in health, fitness, and lifestyle has taken dialogue about ministerial self-stewardship far beyond traditional boundaries. Interestingly enough, a good part of this dialogue involves an attempt to recover a more biblical ethic of the human (ministerial) self.

What biblical guidance is there for a ministerial ethic of self-stewardship?

On the one hand, it has been the new hedonism of the second half of the twentieth century, especially in America, that has pushed society as a whole toward serious interest in physical fitness. On the other hand, there has been a concomitant development of interest in human health and welfare that goes far beyond the body craze. A number of biblical principles bear examination as we look toward the development of a sound "health and welfare" ethic for ministers.

First, the Old Testament is not nearly so body-denying as the Christian church later became. We need not do detailed exegesis of the Song of Solomon in order to conclude that its frank celebration of the physical aspects of romantic love is far more "modern" in spirit than the coldness of much of what has been written and said between then and now. For the writer of the Song, sex and the body are good gifts of God to be celebrated and enjoyed in their proper context rather than denied.

Second, even in primitive times a good deal was known about how to care for one's body so as to produce the best possible results. Much of the background of the Hebrew dietary regulations is a kind of rough-and-ready nutritional good sense. Pork, for example, was a dangerous meat to eat in the days before proper sanitation and cures for trichinosis.

Children's Sunday school classes have often told the story of Daniel as a way of trying to persuade young people to eat their vegetables. The story, of course, is about avoiding ritual defilement rather than practicing good nutrition. Still Daniel 1:8-15 shows that at some level even the ancients were aware of good dietary practices. If you ate by the rules, they believed, God would bless you with strength and good health.

The New Testament evinces little specific concern for Christian stewardship of the body toward good health. Life in the first century was often short and always uncertain, especially for believers. The Christian scriptures were much more concerned with teaching people how to be secure in the next life than healthy in this one.

Having said that, though, we are free to look for what assistance there is. A few Pauline texts do offer some support for personal stewardship. Assuming that the letters to Timothy are genuine, Paul's overall perspective is perhaps best glimpsed in 1 Timothy 4:7b-8.

> Train yourself in godliness, for, while physical training is of some value, godliness is valuable in every way, holding promise for both the present life and the life to come.

The teaching admits a certain benefit to be gained from taking care of one's body in the midst of expressing a clear preference for athletic Christianity. Paul's fatherly concern for Timothy's digestion, "No longer drink only water, but take a little wine for the sake of your stomach and your frequent ailments" (1 Tim 5:23), then provides the opposing motif of placing sensible limits on the early believers' rigorous self-denial.

The Pauline teaching regarding stewardship of the body that has held the most sway in evangelical Protestant life is usually taken out of context and applied with some considerable *eisegesis*. That is found in the clearly genuine Pauline corpus in 1 Corinthians 3:16-17 and 6:19-20.

The former text is found in the midst of Paul's discussion of the factions in the Corinthian church:

> Do you not know that you are God's temple and that God's Spirit dwells in you? If anyone destroys God's temple, God will destroy that person. For God's temple is holy, and you are that temple.

In context it refers to the destructive effects of factionalism within the church and God's jealous guardianship of the spiritual well-being of the believers. In application it has been used to urge Christians to eschew everything from alcohol and tobacco to coconut cream pie.

In fairness, the latter text is a little more to the point. Paul is inveighing against fornication when he argues,

> Or do you not know that your body is a temple of the Holy Spirit within you, which you have from God, and that you are not your own? For you were bought with a price; therefore glorify God in your body.

The reference is legitimately to damage to the body, though again spiritual and not physical damage. The teaching against homosexuality in Romans 1 suggests similar spiritual consequences as do the lists that include gluttony.

It is perhaps more useful in the long run to ask whether there are more general New Testament principles that apply. Is there a discernible, distinctively Christian ethic of self-stewardship? Three possibilities occur. First, the Gospels portray Jesus as particularly concerned with this life and with people's physical health in this life. Why else would so much of his ministry have been devoted to the healing of the sick? If our physical well-being had been unimportant, one could argue, the Master would have spent more of his time and energy teaching people how to cope with their physical infirmities rather than removing them.

Second, in spite of his journey to the cross, Jesus appears to have had a healthy concern for his own welfare. With regularity the Gospels portray him as withdrawing from the crowds for times of solitude, rest, and prayer. When the twelve came back from their first preaching mission, Jesus "took them with him and withdrew privately to a city called Bethsaida" (Luke 9:10). Perhaps he wanted to give them a break from the heavy demands of the crowds!

Third, and most telling, Jesus consistently identified the greatest commandment as

> You shall love the Lord your God with all your heart, and with all your soul, and with all your strength, and with all your mind, and your neighbor as yourself. (Luke 10:27)

While the church has always emphasized the two-thirds of the commandment that refer to love of God and neighbor, it clearly also assumes a healthy love for self. The measure of adequacy for love of one's neighbor is the degree of one's love for self.

Simply put, the Christian ethic as Jesus taught it is self-affirming, self-loving. It does no violence to the Scripture, particularly in the light of the first two principles, to suggest that the third and definitive Christian teaching would be a reasonable concern for one's bodily health and well-being as a part of the truth that we are to *agape* ourselves. It is not surprizing, given the history of the church and the preponderance of teachings regarding self-denial, that this element of self-love has often been submerged to the point of being forgotten. Yet it is present, waiting to be recaptured both for the life of the ministry and for the church as a whole.

How do we determine an ethic of self-stewardship for ministers that makes sense for today?

Ministers today are no longer swimming upstream when it comes to caring for themselves physically and emotionally. Increasingly, judicatories and congregations are recognizing that ministers not only have a right to take care of themselves, but indeed must do so if they are to survive the stresses of the ministry. Even those who have not thought of it yet can be helped to see the benefits of ministerial self-care in terms of performance, job satisfaction, and longevity.

For a young minister such as Brad, with whose waistline we began this section, that should mean that there is a ready potential for teaching his board of deacons or personnel committee about his need for support in his attempts at self-management. From the beginning of conversation with any parish, the minister should discuss expectations and methods regarding self-care. A great deal of this will be dealt with in regard to time management in the last section of this chapter.

Several other matters require attention, however. Health care is a fundamental concern. No church can afford a full-time minister unless it can afford to provide health insurance for the minister and his/her family. With the confusing state of the health insurance industry in the United States, particularly, a clear understanding of the health benefits provided in a church's package should be part of the negotiation for any ministerial position. Nor is it in any way noble or "sacrificial" for a minister to slight himself/herself in this regard because the church budget is tight. It is merely foolish.

The minister and the church should both seek to make the minister's health care package as comprehensive as possible. Dental benefits should be included. No minister should ever accept a package that does not include some form of mental health benefit. The ministry is demonstrably one of the most stressful occupations in the country. It is irresponsible not to provide a way for the minister and the minister's family to get professional counseling should it be needed. Indeed, in relating to ministers I have known, including myself, not needing counseling at some point is a rare experience indeed. My current parish both includes mental health coverage for the whole family as part of my health insurance and provides budget funds for consultation with mental health professionals as the need may arise in the course of ministry.

Mental and spiritual self care should not wait for emergencies, however. Ministers in metropolitan areas frequently form support groups with other ministers for purposes of mutual encouragement and accountability. In general, every minister should have some individual or group other than a spouse with whom he or she can be honest and receive support in personal struggles. To fail to establish such a connection is to risk isolation and to make oneself vulnerable both to illnesses and to temptations.

A second essential part of the minister's self-stewardship is the development and maintenance of a physical fitness regimen. My own routine includes walking and/or weight training at least four days each week. The time involved most days is about forty-five minutes, but the benefits are incalculable in terms of stress management, weight reduction, cardiovascular health, and a general sense of well-being. The practice of walking, particularly, also lends itself to meditation and prayer. Many busy people find that the time during their walk is the best in the day for spiritual exercise. In the days when Glenn Hinson taught at the Southern Baptist Theological Seminary in Louisville, Kentucky, he would walk the three miles from his home to the seminary each day and use that as his quiet time. Being deaf, he would turn off his hearing aids for complete privacy!

Also important in maintaining physical fitness is the development of a regular routine of medical, dental, and vision checkups. Regular checkups are not foolproof guarantees of good health, but they allow early discovery and treatment of problems.

A third element in a healthy self-stewardship is the development of some kind of regular, therapeutic play. The tendency for married male ministers is often to think that their play time is the time they take for sex, but that is a dangerous assumption. It makes one's sex life carry much too heavy a burden. A healthy sex life is a part of self-care, but it should never be the only fun thing we do. Sex is dependent on the emotional availability and health of one's spouse, which in most marriages varies widely in the flow of life.

Many ministers find that a hobby of some kind will fill the bill nicely as a source of play. Anything from golf to woodworking to bird-watching is legitimate, as long as it involves some physical expression, gives pleasure, and does not cost more energy than it generates.

This playing serves to take us out of our regular "ministerial" way of thinking and acting into a different environment, if only for a little while. Because of the perpetual character of the ministerial task, many ministers especially enjoy recreation in which they can actually finish something and thereby gain a sense of accomplishment and completion. Many also enjoy tasks that are specifically physical rather than cerebral. Perhaps the most important aspect of ministerial self-care, however, involves the apportionment of time, which is the subject of the final section of this chapter.

How do I gain control of the time I spend on the job?

It was 3:00 A.M. Saturday now, and Mike was still awake on the lumpy couch in the den. He and Brenda had had their worst fight ever that night—so bad in fact that she had given him an ultimatum.

"You may be married to that church Mike Fishman, but I'm not! And our child won't be either. Either you get your schedule under control so we can have some kind of decent family life, or you get out of the ministry altogether, or I'll get out of this marriage! Do I make myself clear!?" With that she had stomped out of the room, and he had found the bedroom door locked when he tried to follow.

Now his mind was awhirl with anger, self-doubt, and confusion. On the one hand, he knew Brenda was right. He had been neglecting their family life. He did need to work less. Things would have to change if he were going to be any help at all when the baby came. On the other hand, he had been raised to believe the call of God to vocational ministry was absolute, beyond all earthly claims. The ministers' wives he had known growing up had all seemed to accept that and adjust to it. Why couldn't Brenda? Was she becoming a feminist? What if she really left him? What could he do? Maybe he could bring it up in staff meeting this week, although with a workaholic pastor and a growing church, it was hard to see how much could change for the rest of the staff.

He glanced at the clock. It was now 3:20. With a groan he realized he had promised to be at the church for the men's pancake breakfast by

7:30. He punched the pillow, screwed his eyes shut, and turned his face to the wall.

How has the church dealt with
the question of ministerial time management?

Even asking this question of course reflects a distinctly modern, middle class worldview. As long as the Roman church held sway unchallenged, giving oneself to the vocational ministry meant the formal rejection of personal family life and the embrace of a round-the-clock obedience to the demands of the church. That priests worked on the Sabbath was not seen as either unusual or creating any hardship. That's what priests did. Nor have I been able to discover any concept of compensatory time off for rest. Most likely, clergy simply did what was necessary to their task, worked the same dawn-to-dusk hours everyone else did, rested when they were exhausted, and expected nothing else.

That there have always been "worldly," idle clergy is of course indisputable. But it was not until the rise of ministerial family life that the church was presented with a legitimate set of counterbalancing claims on a minister's time. Writing in 1871, the Episcopal clergyman Charles Bridges came down clearly on the side of the ministerial claim. He describes "want of entire devotedness of heart to the Christian ministry" as a defect of personal character.[16]

> We have given ourselves to this work, and we desire to be in it as if there was nothing worth living for besides: it shall form our whole pleasure and delight. We will consecrate our whole time, our whole reading, our whole mind and heart to this service.[17]

The minister's family, Bridges argued, must first be obedient to the minister as ruler of the house. Home must come second in the minister's priorities. Specifically, "All family arrangements [must be] made subordinate to his parochial duties."[18]

Such is the dominant culture of Protestant ministerial family life into the late twentieth century. Whether ministers actually did consistently work to the detriment of their family and personal lives is unmeasurable at this point. According to anecdotal evidence, however, the legacies of broken marriages and alienated children suggest that they did.

Indeed, much of the culture shows little sign of changing. George Barna is one of the most popular "church growth" writers of the 1990s. In his book *Turnaround Churches*, Barna profiles a national sampling of congregations that had been in decline and begun again to grow under new leadership. He argues that one crucial characteristic of those churches was that their pastors worked seventy to eighty hours per week.[19] Barna admits that some might think this is excessive, but argues its necessity if a declining church is to be made healthy again. He does not deal with the impact on the minister's family or personal health and spiritual life, which such a schedule would create.

A more creative but still questionable approach is taken by Ruth Truman in her 1974 book, *Underground Manual for Ministers' Wives.* Speaking from personal experience as a Methodist minister's daughter and wife, Truman good-humoredly accepts the cultural defintions of a minister's time commitments and counsels women (this was 1974, remember) on how to have a decent life with their minister husbands in spite of the time demands. In a chapter on sex, for example, she argues,

> Flexibility is the key to parsonage sex life. . . . An afternoon house call from your favorite minister-husband might be the solution—or morning coffee break. You don't really have to drink the coffee.[20]

Truman is fun reading, but she never really deals with the question of whether the minister's schedule ought to be the place where change begins. In fact, she goes the other way:

> All other things aside, when you give your husband love you must also give him freedom—even to work himself to death if that is his choice. Set him free to do his thing. He only gets one life, so why not let him live it the way he feels is right for him?[21]

This cheerful surrender to the time demands of ministry as inevitable begs the question entirely.

By the 1950s, however, at least at the level of academic study of the profession, change was beginning to come to the way a minister's time was seen. As the country as a whole moved toward the forty-hour work week and the ministry began to be seen more as a profession, many ministers, especially in the mainline churches, began to observe a day off in each week as a part of their regular discipline. In a volume he edited on *The Minister's Own Mental Health,* Wayne Oates, distinguished professor of pastoral care, holds that "The mythical 'day off' is really a mirage! Many times the minister will work three or four weeks without a day off."[22] At the same time he argues for accruing days off toward frequent short trips out of town and for managing the minister's day so as to provide time for self and family.

The same volume begins to recognize the legitimacy of the claims of the minister's family. Wallace Denton observed, "When asked what she dislikes most about being a minister's wife, her answer is likely to be lack of family time."[23] The significant difference from earlier works is that he treats the wife's claims on her husband's time as right and proper in the context of marriage, and declares that the solution is "a healthy dose from her husband of love, attention, and time."[24]

By the 1980s, it was well established in the professional literature that ministers must set limits to the time they will work. We quote at some length from a volume edited by the British Methodist Cyril Rodd:

> The first [pastoral priority] is to set boundaries to our work time. This is the hardest step of all, and many pastors will recoil from it. Yet without it, there is no way in which we can begin to talk about priorities. Setting limits to the time we spend at work need not prevent us from being available to people in their need. No minister can or would want to exclude the possibility of leisure being interrupted by emergencies or unforseen events. (Though we do need time which is free even from the possibility of interruption and must take care to arrange this also.) What we can do is set limits to the time in which we are prepared to contemplate forseen events. This will both enable us to feel positive toward leisure and will compel us to face the need to choose priorities. It will also enable us to have time for those we need most, our families and closest friends.[25]

With typical British reserve, the author declines to get more specific than this.

American Methodists, however, have not been so shy. The Methodist R. Franklin Gillis, Jr., wrote an entire volume typical of the growing concern for how ministers best order their time.[26] Such volumes typically major on time management techniques without being prescriptive about how much time a minister ought to work in a given week or how to achieve a reasonable schedule. Gillis does seem to suggest that sixty hours is a reasonable maximum for ministers to work. Beyond that he simply tries to help ministers make the best use of whatever time they choose to spend. The next step for our inquiry is to ask whether there are biblical helps available for this peculiarly modern problem of the minister's time management.

How does scripture inform
an ethic of time management for ministers?

The first thing to realize, of course, is that, contrary to the last statement in the paragraph above, time management is not a peculiarly modern problem at all. It is so engrained a part of the challenge of being human that the rhythm of the days is established by commandment:

> Six days you shall labor and do all your work. But the seventh day is a sabbath to the Lord your God; you shall not do any work–you, your son or your daughter, your male or female slave, your livestock, or the alien resident in your towns. For in six days the Lord made heaven and earth, the sea, and all that is in them, but rested the seventh day; therefore the Lord blessed the seventh day and consecrated it. (Exod 20:9-11)

Some commentators think the taboo on work actually preceeded the religious aspects of the day, that the primitive Hebrews instinctively recognized they could not work without rest.

This fundamental recognition is more important than one might suppose. Our holiest code both clearly recognizes the need for and builds into the structure of the flow of time itself a universal provision for rest.

The important point for our study is that rest was seen at the very beginning of Judeo-Christian development as an essential component in time management. The time poem in Ecclesiastes 3 suggests, similarly, that the Hebrews were both conscious of and sophisticated about the flow of time in our lives. The preacher says:

> I have seen the business that God has given to everyone to be busy with. He has made everything suitable for its time; moreover he has put a sense of past and future into their minds. . . . I know that there is nothing better for them than to be happy and enjoy themselves as long as they live; moreover, it is God's gift that all should eat and drink and take pleasure in all their toil. (vv. 10-13)

To the concept of a time for rest the preacher adds the idea of recreation, enjoyment as the appropriate product of human work. He warns against working too hard:

> What do mortals get from all the toil and strain with which they toil under the sun? For all their days are full of pain, and their work is a vexation; even at night their minds do not rest. This also is vanity. (2:22-23)

Throughout Ecclesiastes the theme of enjoyment reappears as the best that can be expected from human work.

Ecclesiastes thus serves as an excellent corrective to the other major stream of Old Testament teaching regarding work, what produces "the Protestant work ethic." The pithy sayings of Proverbs rather than the jaded cynicism of Ecclesiastes have dominated Western Christianity. Admonitions such as "A little sleep, a little slumber, a little folding of the hands to rest, and poverty will come upon you like a robber, and want, like an armed warrior" (Prov 24:33-34) along with the story of the industry of the ant found their way into Western thought with a vigor that the preacher's cynicism lacked.

The result is that, rather than embracing an ethic of appropriate leisure, Western culture has spent much of its energy urging one another to ever greater efforts at earning money. No less a figure than John Wesley is reported to have admonished "Make all you can! Save all you can!" That he then added "Give all you can!" somehow seems easily forgotten. This is the weakness of capitalist philosophy. Rather than recognizing that all labor has appropriate limits, we have spent much of the twentieth century trying to find ways around Sabbath restrictions—in the United States apparently mainly for the sake of opening Wal Mart on Sunday.

On one level Jesus appears to have contributed to a distortion of biblical balance regarding labor. His constant conflict with Pharisaic legalism played itself out in part in a battle over their perversion of the Sabbath rest. In resisting their legalism, he argues in Matthew 12:5 that "on the sabbath the priests in the temple break the sabbath and yet are guiltless." He then goes on to argue that any "good" activity may be lawful.

> Suppose one of you has only one sheep and it falls into a pit on the sabbath; will you not lay hold of it and lift it out? How much more valuable is a human being than a sheep! So it is lawful to do good on the sabbath. (vv. 11-12).

The Master thus gives both specific approval to clergy work on the day of worship and a general approbation to any kind of good works. Unfortunately for the clergy, there is no equally specific blessing given for clergy rest. Indeed the task of the kingdom is portrayed as so urgent and demanding that people abandon normal life in order to pursue it.

> To another he said, "Follow me." But he said, "Lord, first let me go and bury my father." But Jesus said to him, "Let the dead bury their

own dead; but as for you, go and proclaim the kingdom of God." Another said, "I will follow you, Lord; but let me first say farewell to those at my home." Jesus said to him, "No one who puts a hand to the plow and looks back is fit for the kingdom of God." (Luke 9:59-62)

This repeated theme of the urgency and primacy of kingdom work underlies the concept of Christian vocation and produces the modern idea that clergy should be about kingdom work whether or not it is good for them and their families. Clergy spouses, until recently usually wives, are frequently heard to complain "I cannot compete with the church!" Even knowing that patterns of excessive work are harmful, neither clergy nor their families feel able to resist what they perceive as the imperative of kingdom work, especially since Jesus himself appears to be the source of the imperative!

Nor does the remainder of the New Testament offer much help. Paul's heroic Christianity, the stories of the early churches, and John's call for faithfulness in the face of persecution appear to lend support to the culture of clergy sacrifice as it would develop in later years.

This is a case in which we must return to basic concepts of biblical interpretation. When the Scripture appears to be in conflict, or when we have questions about specific interpretations, we turn to the life and witness of Jesus for clarification. Only by doing so do we begin to see some clarity with regard to the issue of the use of clergy time.

First, we must remember that Jesus was not teaching for a clergy situation analogous to our own. Whether he was mistaken about the nearness of the end or he has simply been misrepresented, his teachings about the urgency of kingdom work come from the perspective of a very short time in which to accomplish God's purposes. They are designed to get the attention of those who fail to give attention to God's call.

Second, with regard to the ordinary work of life—the professional, "making a living" aspect of our existence—Jesus' teachings give a very different perspective. His call to "consider the lilies of the field" could be said to apply to the work of a minister just as much as to that of a stockbroker. The parable of the rich fool (Luke 12:13-21) gains a whole new meaning if the "treasure" is seen as a church's budget and the "barns" as its new state-of-the-art sanctuary. To the extent that the minister, though engaged in kingdom work, yet lives in ordinary time with all the entanglements and commitments ordinary time entails, professional ministry must be governed by the same cautions and restraints with which Christians are advised to approach any other profession.

We must also remember that Jesus himself, though engaged in the most important kingdom work of all, both took frequent times of retreat from his work and gained the reputation of someone who enjoyed the good things of life. His own life argues against the narrow, single-minded asceticism that has sometimes both characterized the work of the clergy and been seen as the clerical ideal.

That Paul recognized the demands that marriage and family life place upon one is evident from his discussion of marriage in 1 Corinthians 7. Following Jesus, he expected an early end to the present age. He advised those unmarried and married to remain so. But he argued that the unmarried are better off because of the demands of marriage. He was not speaking of clergy but simply of the members of the church. Yet he saw himself as more free to do the work of an apostle because he was not married, and thought it well that others be as he.

The New Testament Scriptures thus live in tension between the urgency of the kingdom and the importance of everyday life. The minister's ethic of time management is informed by this tension and made more difficult as the minister attempts to balance kingdom imperatives and professional realities. It remains to attempt to draw some conclusions.

How should individual ministers balance their personal and professional time?

First, there is no magic solution to the dilemma of the professional minister. By its very nature, the job of ministry will absorb as much time as a minister will give it. Many ministers work sixty- or seventy-hour weeks and still feel a tremendous sense of inadequacy about their performance. There will always be one more phone call that can be made or visit that can be paid.

Without attempting to set a specific time goal, Cecil Sherman, in an unpublished address at Georgetown College, Georgetown, Kentucky, 17 April 1995, argued that the pastor should strive for a "grade" of "B" in church and a grade of "B" in family. What Dr. Sherman meant is that a married minister will never be able to meet all the demands of a church because of the time that must be reserved for family; nor will a married minister be able to meet all the demands of family because of the heavy time commitments church requires. Living in tension is a necessary part of the professional ministerial milieu.

We should remember, however, that except for jobs with a specific hourly prescription, all professionals deal with this same kind of tension.

It is no more appropriate for the minister to advise her banker friends to make their family a priority, while she neglects her own, than it is for the minister to advise sexual fidelity while he is himself unfaithful to his vows. What can we say then about the minister's time?

First, it is very helpful to press church personnel and administrative committees to define the hourly expectations of the minister's job description. They will be reluctant to do this. Many will believe instinctively that the minister should be on twenty-four hour call. And most ministers are. At the same time, all ministers deserve a clear definition of the hours they are expected to work, days off that may be taken each week, and how vacation time and compensatory time are accrued. If the laborers are worthy of their hire, they are also worthy of knowing what is expected of them and when they may legitimately take time off.

Two items deserve further comment. Because of the erratic flow of ministerial work, an understanding about compensatory time off is a vital part of every ministerial contract. When you have just spent 120 hours straight with the middle schoolers on retreat, it makes little sense to show up the next morning at 9:00 for office hours. Ministers need to be freed to adjust their schedules to compensate for frequently necessary long hours.

In addition, there is a little-noticed loss that ministerial families suffer because of the location of Sunday in the weekly calendar. In the United States in the 1990s, there are a number of three-day-long weekends created by federal holidays that are routinely observed on Monday. These long weekends have become part of the rhythm of American life and provide much-needed breaks in the regular flow of work for many families. Ministerial families never get them. Sunday must still be observed. Very few churches have written into their ministerial contracts any kind of "weekend guarantee" for their ministerial families. But for many families it is precisely that kind of short break in routine that provides time for stress-relief and fun.

A second critical point is that all ministers must take responsibility for managing their own use of time. The Jesus who assumes that we will love ourselves no doubt expects us to practice that self-love in the most practical and concrete kinds of ways, just as he took care of himself in the midst of the flow of his own work. Time away from the crowds and time for play are essential for us just as they were for him. And the fact that he did not have a family, while most of us Protestants do, does not excuse us neglecting our families and citing Jesus as our model.

Precisely how do ministers decide responsibly how much time to work and where to draw the line? The best suggestion I have seen appeared in *The Minister's Own Mental Health*, to which I referred earlier. The suggestion is that ministers take their calendars and divide each week into twenty-one periods—morning, afternoon, and evening for each of the seven days. Those of us in the professional ministry expect as part of the territory that we will often work when others do not. Evenings and weekends are often the time when our people are most available to us. At the same time with more ministerial spouses working outside the home, and especially with school-age children, our own family time must also come evenings and weekends. Ministers should therefore design their calendars so as to work no more than thirteen of the twenty-one periods in a typical week.

The number of periods actually worked in a given week should also serve as a guide in deciding how much compensatory time off should be taken the next week. Certain seasons of the year require extra time commitments. Advent, Holy Week, revival services, and other special events will sometimes require almost round-the-clock involvement. Those seasons should be followed as soon as possible by extra time off. By recognizing the special demands of ministerial life and designing one's flow of work accordingly, careful ministers should be able to make Dr. Sherman's "B" in family.

To some, the suggestions of this chapter will sound as though I am trying to define away the special demands of the ministerial calling. On the contrary, my intention is to point out that the same demands of stewardship that ministers continually hold out as goals for their parishioners apply in their own lives as well. The writer of 1 Timothy (3:1-7) makes it clear that one of the primary qualifications for church leadership is an exemplary family life. And no minister can have a good family life who spends all of his/her time and energy at work.

Notes

[1] Wilhelm Pauck, "The Ministry in the Time of the Continental Reformation," in *The Ministry in Historical Perspectives*, H. Richard Niebuhr and Daniel D. Williams, eds. (San Francisco: Harper & Row, 1983) 146.

[2] Margaret H. Watt, *The History of the Parson's Wife* (London: Faber and Faber Ltd., 1943) 7-27. This obscure but fascinating monograph tells the story of the development of the institution of clergy marriage in England in vivid detail.

[3] Ibid., 8.

[4]George Herbert, "The Country Parson," in George Herbert, *The Country Parson, The Temple,* John N. Wall, Jr., ed. (New York: Paulist Press, 1981) 68-69.

[5]Dorothy Harrison Pentecost, *The Pastor's Wife and the Church* (Chicago: Moody Press) 45ff.

[6]Lucille Lavender, *They Cry, Too! What You Always Wanted to Know about Your Minister But Didn't Know Whom to Ask* (Grand Rapids MI: Zondervan, 1986) 89.

[7]David and Vera Mace, *What's Happening to Clergy Marriages* (Nashville: Abingdon, 1980).

[8]Ibid., 37.

[9]For a deeper look at this issue from a biblical perspective, consult *Woman in the World of Jesus, Frank and Evelyn Stagg* (Philadelphia: Westminster, 1978).

[10]Mace, 51.

[11]George H. Williams, "The Ministry in the Ante-Nicene Church," in *The Ministry in Historical Perspective*, 54.

[12]Pauck, 143.

[13]Ibid., 144-45.

[14]Winthrop S. Hudson, "The Ministry in the Puritan Age," in *The Ministry in Historical Perspective*, 183.

[15]Ibid., 184.

[16]Charles Bridges, *The Christian Ministery* (New York: Robert Carter and Brothers, 1871) 102-107.

[17]Ibid., 102.

[18]Ibid., 157.

[19]George Barna, *Turnaround Churches* (Ventura CA: Regal Books, 1993).

[20]Ruth Truman, *Underground Manual for Ministers' Wives* (Nashville: Abingdon, 1974) 41.

[21]Ibid., 38.

[22]Wayne E. Oates, "The Healthy Minister," in *The Minister's Own Mental Health* (Great Neck NY: Channel Press, Inc., 1961) 16.

[23]Wallace Denton, "Role Attitudes of the Minister's Wife," in *The Minister's Own Mental Health*, 175.

[24]Ibid., 178.

[25]J. David Bridge, "The Pastor's Priorities," in *The Pastor's Problems*, Cyril Rood, ed. (Edinburgh: T. & T. Clark Ltd., 1985) 4.

[26]R. Franklin Gillis, Jr., It's About Time: Time Management for Church Professionals (Lima OH: C.S.S., 1989).

Part 2
The Public Sphere

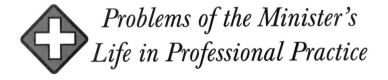

Problems of the Minister's Life in Professional Practice

CHAPTER 4

AUTHORITY

The trouble with getting your private life as a minister in order is that you have yet to enter the door of the church. That public world of pulpit and committee room and hospital requires equally exact ethical navigation. So we look now at central issues of the ministry in the public sphere.

Where do I get my authority?

It's Sunday morning. The average congregation ambles in, claims its accustomed pew, nods cordially to its neighbors, and waits for you, its minister, to mount the pulpit and do what is normally done.

The question is, "Why?" Why are they willing to listen to you for twenty or thirty or (heaven forbid) forty minutes? What right do you have to speak to them? What right do you have to expect them to take seriously what you say? What is the basis of your ministerial authority? How do you work that authority out in your day-to-day relationship with the congregation you serve?

Even these days some still see the minister as a figure of tremendous authority. The theologian Bernard Ramm defined authority in the religious sense as

> that right or power to command action or compliance, or to determine belief or custom, expecting obedience from those under authority, and in return giving responsible account for the claim to right or power.[1]

Many of us would feel immediately that Ramm claims too much. The power to command obedience feels like more than a minister ought to have. Indeed, the nature of late-twentieth-century ministry is such that many of us would feel we had acquired the tongues of angels if we could only be confident our congregations are listening to what we say on Sunday mornings, much less that they would obey.

But if we choose to reject Ramm, either deciding his definition is impractical or biblically and theologically wrong, we still must decide what claim to authority is right for our ministry. As a practical matter, if nothing else, every minister has to have some basis for operation. So when you step into the pulpit and open your mouth, or when you lie awake and think about what you will say next time, where do you get your authority? Is there an adequate historical, biblical, and theological rationale for ministerial authority? If so, what should the nature of that authority be?

What are the historical bases for ministerial authority?

Historically, of course, the church has operated under two primary models of authority. The first, hammered out in the long centuries of Roman Catholic preeminence and culminating in the nineteenth-century doctrine of papal infallibility, is the hierarchical model. Ministers in the hierarchical tradition knew their place. They were set apart from and above the laity. Ordination made them brother priests with the pope and with Christ himself. Still they operated as cogs in a more or less efficient ecclesiastical machine. Their job was to baptize, to catechize, to marry, to bury, and to carry out the instructions that came to them from above.

Authority centered in the hierarchy of the priesthood as the prime interpreters of scripture and tradition. Armed with the aid of the Holy Spirit, which descended from the apostles by the laying on of hands, the hierarchy spoke for God, mediating God's grace to humankind. The flow of command was downward from the pope as Christ's vicar through archbishop and bishop and priest to the people. Each found salvation by living as an obedient child of the church. Thus the priest in his parish actually approached the authority of Ramm's definition.

Non-Catholic hierarchical churches either found their authority in an alternative bishop, such as the patriarch of Constantinople for the Eastern Orthodox, or in a marriage of church and state as in Anglicanism. The Mormon sect in America is one of the most interesting modern imitations of this essentially medieval pattern.

Even today, for ministers who accept its presuppositions, hierarchicalism provides a relatively effective structure for ministry. While it has never operated quite so efficiently as our summary suggests, and while Roman Catholicism, for example, began to move toward substantial changes with Vatican II, hierarchicalism remains the structure of authority for two-thirds of the world's Christian ministers.

These days, however, hierarchical authority in ministry seems sometimes to operate most clearly in its breach. In San Diego,

California, in 1989, a Roman Catholic bishop excommunicated a woman of his diocese when she campaigned for the state senate with an openly pro-choice stand on abortion. Though she had been trailing till the bishop's announcement, she promptly won the election. That clearly was not what the bishop intended. In the same vein, many Catholics simply ignore the Church's teachings on birth control and marital relations. Indeed, those priests and bishops who seem to have the most effective authority with Catholic people in the United States are those who work to soften the harshest effects of their church's decrees.

The first serious challenge to the hierarchical model for ministerial authority, the second great stream of thinking about ministerial authority in Christian history, emerged with the Protestant Reformation. Obviously Martin Luther could not support the idea of a ministerial hierarchy culminating in absolute papal authority while he himself defied the pope. Nor could the radical Anabaptists support Luther's modified state church when Luther accused them of undermining the very fabric of society. As a consequence, ministers in the Reformation period and after sought new bases for their authority. These took two primary forms.

The same reformers who argued that faith alone could secure salvation also argued that scripture alone could instruct the Christian life. They made the Bible, available for the first time in the peoples' languages, a kind of paper pope. Reformation ministers began to justify their positions on the basis that they were more "biblical" than those of their opponents. This claim to biblical authority has been absolutely crucial to Protestant ministry ever since.

In the 1970s, Missouri Synod Lutherans split over the claim that some more liberal ministers and professors had strayed from a strict commitment to biblical authority. Odd as it sounds to some from other traditions, Southern Baptists in the 1990s approached a de facto split centering theologically on a debate whether the Bible is merely authoritative and functionally infallible in the life of the believer or is also historically and scientifically inerrant in the (admittedly nonexistent) original manuscripts.

Interestingly, the most conservative, literalist interpretations of scripture, at least in evangelical life, have tended to correlate with higher views of the authority of the individual minister. A resolution passed at the 1988 Southern Baptist Convention, which was dominated by the convention's literalist faction, blunted traditional commitment to "the priesthood of the believer" in favor of "the authority of the pastor."[2] Similarly, the shepherding movement among charismatics gives ministers substantial control over the lives of their people, even to the point of forbidding specific marriages and controlling career choices. A kind of patriarchal biblical hierarchicalism taught by independent seminar leaders such as Bill Gothard seeks to place all relationships in a male-dominated structure from pastor to father to husband. In this latter approach, of course, women are gender-ineligible for the ministry.

At one extreme, then, this claim to biblical authority for ministry seeks to recreate patriarchal, first-century Jewish and Christian society in a modern context. Life goes back to a simpler, less complicated era. We recreate a hierarchical claim to obedience without an elaborate hierarchy. One aspect of this approach is a special emphasis on traditional family values that has great appeal to many people. That a traditionalist view of scripture necessarily leads to a healthy family life is logically obscure, but the connection in many people's minds is very real. In debate on the ordination of women to the diaconate, I heard one minister say such a move would lead directly to the breakdown of the family and the rise of homosexuality.

Whether the Bible's teachings actually take us in this authoritarian direction will be discussed in the next major section of this chapter. I believe a serious attitude toward biblical teachings leads us to quite a different view of the minister's authority, one that is not dependent on particular family structures or cultural values.

The second primary form Protestant justification of ministerial authority has taken is derived from the doctrine of the priesthood of the believer. Protestants argued on the basis of the New Testament that in Christ each of us is responsible to manage our own relationship with God. In the congregation, then, the collective will of the body becomes the best determinant of God's will and the best root for authority. Luther held that when a bishop consecrates a new minister he is simply acting on behalf of the congregation. He taught that a priest could be both chosen and dismissed by the people and said that choice could be made on the basis of whether and how well the minister preached the true gospel.[3]

Since Luther, normal practice in most of the free churches has been for ministers to be chosen by congregational consent and to derive much of their working authority from that choice. In late twentieth-century America, pragmatism has led to a new wrinkle in evangelical life. Americans have always had a cultural bent toward pragmatism: "If it works, do it. If it doesn't, fix it!" The result is many ministers find their authority with their congregations waxing or waning as their ministry is judged on the basis of its effectiveness. The more effective the ministry, the more authority the minister is given.

California religious life, in particular, has been transformed in the past decade by the emergence of a model of ministry typified by the Saddleback Valley Community Church of southern California. Begun from scratch by one minister with a dream of reaching non-churched baby boomers, Saddleback quickly grew to several thousand members. Saddleback and churches like it have grown largely under the positive, pragmatic, personal leadership of one minister operating as a kind of corporate chief executive officer. Along the way at Saddleback, the pastor tossed out most traditional structure, liturgy, and music as ineffective with the church's target audience. He geared Saddleback's ministries and worship specifically to the segment of the population born between 1946 and 1964. For example, even though the church came from Baptist roots, they quickly dropped the monthly decision-making or "business" session of the whole congregation in favor of a yearly stockholders'-type meeting.

Just as nothing succeeds like success, so also nothing in a pragmatic culture makes a more persuasive claim to authority than effectiveness. Increasingly in evangelical circles ministers unwilling to drop traditional liturgy or to trade the hymnody for more contemporary music find their leadership brought into question on the basis of an appeal to effectiveness. Those who attract large numbers by whatever means are appealed to as were the archbishops in days of old. The priesthood of the believer becomes not so much an appeal to the leadership of all by the Spirit as an appeal to what seems to be most popular at the moment. The minister gets authority by giving the people what they want whether what they want is biblically and theologically sound or not.

The priesthood of the believer also operates, of course, in congregations with the opposite problem. Some are so loyal to a tradition or a language or a particular group's hold on power that nothing changes and nothing gets done. They refuse to adapt to changing ministry situations, and they die. Ministers in these churches have authority only as tenders of the sacred flame.

This sketch by no means exhausts the ways ministers seek to authenticate their ministries, but it does suggest something of the range of approaches and of the depth of the problem. Each traditional approach has its benefits. Each is subject to manipulation and abuse. As I entered my first pastorate in a little country church in Kentucky, I knew the crucial issue of my ministry there would be whether and how I could lead the church, not just to elect me, but also to accept me as their pastor. Coming from a tradition that combined strong allegiances to biblical authority and to the priesthood of the believer, I had to ask further, "Could I gain authority in a way that was biblically acceptable to me and that paid proper attention to the people's dignity in Christ?" In other words, "Is there one best biblical/theological model for ministerial authority?" Next, then, we shall look for such a model.

What are the biblical/ theological bases for ministerial authority?

The two most prominent New Testament images for ministerial authority are those that form the roots of our English words "pastor" and "minister." Pastor is actually used only in Ephesians 4:11 as Paul describes the gifts of the Spirit to be used in the upbuilding of the church. Its Greek root, however, derives from the concept of shepherding used by Jesus to describe himself in his relationship with the disciples. Thus we have a ready picture for the nature of the pastoral task: "I am the good shepherd. The good shepherd lays down his life for the sheep" (John 10:11). In fact, most of the tenth chapter of John focuses on this image of the shepherd in the homely, day-to-day tasks of caring for the sheep, teaching them to recognize his voice, rescuing them from danger, putting himself even in danger of death to protect them from wild animals and thieves.

Clearly the correspondence between a modern minister's experiences and those of Jesus is not one-to-one. Our good shepherd died once for all. We have already spoken about some of the practical limits on ministerial commitment placed by prior obligations to family. Yet the image is still valid. Many a minister has given the talents and energies of a lifetime for the welfare of those of Christ's sheep in his or her charge. My own home pastor has served in my family's town for well over a quarter of a century now. He has had many opportunities to move onward and upward to larger, more prestigious posts. But he has chosen to give himself for that one church, that one sheepfold. He has not suffered martyrdom, but he has quite literally laid down his life nonetheless.

The shepherd in the New Testament is thus an authority whose influence is used for one purpose and one purpose alone: the welfare of the sheep. If this were the only New Testament picture we had, however, we still would not have a satisfactory picture of the nature of ministerial authority. A shepherd, after all, can be quite arbitrary and demanding in relating to the sheep. Some ministers, in fact, use the shepherding image to claim that right on the basis of their sacrifice.

It takes a second New Testament image to round out the picture. The root for our word minister is the Greek *diakonos*, variously translated deacon, deaconess, servant, or minister. Paul wrote repeatedly of his status as a servant of the church. The much-maligned Phoebe of the church at Cenchrae in Romans 16:2 was either a deacon or deaconess or servant or minister, depending on the particular translator's bias.

The determinative passage for the character and authority of Christian servanthood (and thus, I would claim, of Christian ministry) comes in the Synoptics as Christ responds to the disciples' disputes over which of them is the greatest. In the Matthean account,

> Jesus called them to him and said, "You know that the rulers of the Gentiles lord it over them, and their great ones are tyrants over them. It will not be so among you; but whoever wishes to be great among you must be your servant, and whoever wishes to be first among you must be your slave; just as the Son of Man came not to be served but to serve, and to give his life a ransom for many. (20:25-28)

Clearly, among the disciples of Christ, servanthood—even slavery *(doulos)*—to the welfare of all is the criterion by which authority is earned. There are a host of other images of the minister in Paul's writings: the father to children, the nurse to an infant, the teacher to students, the example to imitators, and so on. None, however, is as explicit and definitive as the image of servanthood. The literature, moreover, suggests broad agreement on this interpretation. The Roman Catholic Hans Küng says it perhaps as well as anyone:

> It is not law or power, knowledge or dignity which is the basis of discipleship. The model is not . . . even the priest who stands above his people, the only valid model is that of a man who serves tables.[4]

In other words, ministry is simply a vocational extension of discipleship. It carries with it no inherent authority except that which the minister earns—that which is ascribed to the minister by a congregation as he or she serves them.

On the basis of these biblical images, it seems that the moral orientation of the self of the Christian minister, the minister's character, should be the character of servanthood. In some ways the biblical formulation, if we choose to follow it, renders the question of how the minister achieves authority obsolete, at least to the degree that we accept Ramm's definition of authority as power that commands obedience. One simply cannot seek power for oneself at the same time one seeks to be a servant of Christ's people. The two movements are in opposite directions. To this degree all claims of ministerial authority, especially those that give the pastor sole decision-making responsibility in the church or that create between minister and people a flow of power from the top down, must be seen as *prima facie* unbiblical.

Where does authority in the church lie? It lies with the risen Christ. Philippians 2:5-11 is the key passage: "He humbled himself and became obedient to the point of death—even death on a cross. Therefore God also highly exalted him." The same Christ who said, "The Son of man came not to be served but to serve" also said after the resurrection, "All authority in heaven and on earth has been given to me." Clearly we ministers are not the risen Christ, even though some of us have a tendency to act as though we think we are. Even so, the concept of the authority of the risen Christ has the unmistakable air of the church triumphant. Resurrection authority smacks of command, and ministers might be forgiven for seeking in their status as representatives of Christ some justification for a more aggressive stance than servanthood by itself suggests. We might even be forgiven for asking how, from a posture of servanthood, we are ever supposed to get anything done.

Perhaps the best question to ask here is "What is the point of the minister's authority?" Christ stated it at the same time he claimed authority for himself: "Go therefore and make disciples." The object of life for Christian ministers is to spread the gospel of Christ. The criterion for evaluating ministerial authority must therefore be the test of whether the whole gospel both in its sense of salvation and in its sense of the abundant life is being served. The elements of that test in a given situation will be as specific and as varied as the gospel itself.

In effect, the Christian minister gains authority through serving as that service proves to meet the needs of Christ's church. The authority given by their congregations to the pastors of Willow Creek Community Church in Illinois and Saddleback Valley Community Church in southern California must be seen as appropriate on the basis of the test of the effectiveness of their leadership in spreading the gospel. Their authority will ultimately prove invalid only if their approach somehow eventually betrays the gospel it is intended to serve.

For those of us in more traditional settings, testing our authority on the basis of our service to the gospel may use other criteria than that of reaching the baby boomers. Sometimes, of course, a minister who appears to be effectively serving the church and extending the gospel will lose all authority on the basis of a personal failure. Not long ago a pastor I knew was discovered to be involved in an affair of longstanding with the wife of a staff member. His authority in his congregation as well as his influence in his denomination vanished overnight. His behavior betrayed the gospel he claimed to serve. Interestingly, when confronted, he begged to go on being pastor! The lay board of the church had to say his actions had lost him their trust.

The check that will keep any minister, in the free church tradition at least, from exceeding his or her proper authority is thus the one that Luther recognized: the priesthood of the believer. Perhaps Pastor Jones, who has been serving Bayside Church for five years, becomes convinced that the church needs to expand its ministry for Christ remodeling and enlarging its facilities, thus presenting a more attractive and accommodating image to its community. She begins pushing hard for a building project.

In the free church tradition such decisions are made by the congregation. The church does not simply go along with Pastor Jones. The members begin to evaluate the proposal for themselves. "Do I agree with Pastor's assessment of our situation? Do I think we need a better image in our community? Do I believe this project will help us achieve a more effective witness? Is this the best thing we can do right now to serve Christ here in our town?"

If the congregation agrees with the pastor's assessment, they move toward their common goal. If not, they do not adopt the proposal on the basis of the pastor's authority. They seek another way together. Such evaluations, obviously, are always subjective. They depend upon the people involved, the facts of the situation, and the leadership of the Holy Spirit. The claim of faith is, if his people listen, Christ will always lead them in the proper way. Ministers who focus their servanthood on making, teaching, supporting, and upbuilding disciples and the church will find their authority confirmed. This observation leads to the final, practical question of this section.

How do ministers gain the
authority necessary for the practice of ministry?

Let us go back to my first pastorate in rural Kentucky, a two-hundred-year-old church in a stable community with a long history of seminary student pastors who stayed a year or two then moved on to bigger and better things. I was full of new ideas and untried strategies, but how could I gain authority? How could I get congregational support for my ministry, especially in a church whose history had taught them not to put too much stock in any one pastor?

I had not developed a theology of servanthood then, but I had been given some good advice. A pastor hero of mine named John Claypool had once told me something like, "You earn the right to speak. You visit the sick and the unchurched. You baptize and marry and bury; and, in that process, family by family, the church gives you their trust." So I began, not by trying bold initiatives, but by concentrating on the details of servanthood. As it happened, the process of earning authority in that congregation was shortened considerably by a situation that already existed in the church. Sunday school teacher Ya, the wife of deacon Yb, was known by practically the entire community to be engaged in an extramarital affair with property chairman Xb, the husband of Sunday school director Xa. Both X's and both Y's sang in the eight-person choir.

The process of discovering, confronting and coping with the aftermath of that situation robbed me of any energy for innovation. Yet it made me pastor of that congregation in a way that only ministering through such a crisis could have done. I became, forever in their memories, "the pastor who handled the affair." Extraordinary service, which by the way I did not choose and would have done anything short of resigning to avoid, led to extraordinary authority. They would have been willing to try almost anything I suggested. Had that crisis not arisen, my tenure would have been much like that of many others, a long, slow struggle to win respect.

The slow path to authority through servanthood is the norm in ministry. As Karl Barth wrote, "There can be privileges and claims and dignities only in and with the duties and obligations of service."[5] For most of us, most of the time, ministerial authority—never in the sense of command, but rather in the sense of influence and the right to be heard and taken seriously—will be gained over time as we build and maintain a relationship of trust with the congregations we serve. From first to last, that relationship must be built around the minister's identity as servant of the church for the sake of Jesus Christ.

This servanthood exists in tension, not only with the minister's private life, but also with the professional aspects of the ministerial vocation and with the natural desire of any leader to get things done. Professionally, we ministers have always been at a disadvantage because that very servanthood that wins us respect tends to work against us in setting up a fair employment contract with a church. How can you keep the posture of a servant and demand two days a week off or four weeks a year vacation time? In the next part of this chapter we shall explore more thoroughly the relationship between servanthood and professionalism. We shall do so by examining the ethics of setting up and maintaining a ministerial contract with a specific congregation.

How can I negotiate a congregational contract?

When I went to that first little congregation in the Kentucky countryside, the hiring process was typical for churches of my denomination. On the basis of my resumé, I was interviewed by the pastor search committee. On the basis of the interview, the committee arranged to hear me preach in a neighboring congregation. Liking what they heard (I suppose), the search committee then arranged for me to preach the Sunday morning sermon at the church "in view of a call." I preached, the church voted, and that was that. I was the pastor.

In all that process, except for my resumé, no piece of paper changed hands. Expectations were discussed, of course, but none were written down. No salary figures, no benefits, no holidays, no ministry duties, nothing of what I was actually to do was specified in writing. No one saw any need. They knew what a pastor was supposed to do, and so did I. Or so we all thought.

A couple of weeks later the real expectations started to surface. "Mrs. N and Mrs. Z need to be visited, Pastor. No, they haven't been to church in five years. Yes, they are perfectly healthy. Well, Pastor T three pastors ago made them angry, but they might come if you would go." "Mrs. O is a shut-in, Pastor. She is so lonely. I know you're just part-time, but surely you could visit her once a week!" "Since your house is next door to the church, would you mind helping us keep the church lawn mowed?"

In the secular employment world it is assumed that any employment arrangement involves some sort of contract, not always but preferably written, in which the parties agree what hours will be worked, what tasks will be performed, and for what wages and benefits. Such a contract delineates specific goals and directions for the job. Very few would be silly enough to begin employment without such an agreement. Yet in the ministry it is at least as common to enter a relationship with a congregation without such an agreement as with one. The results are thwarted ministry, misunderstanding, bitterness, ministerial burnout, and unmet congregational expectations. Most of us would like to know, of course, "Can we avoid poisoning our ministerial relationships, maintain our attitude of servanthood, and protect ourselves from unrealistic expectations all at the same time?" We begin by looking briefly at the historical background of the issue.

How have ministerial contracts been achieved in the past?

In the hierarchical churches the tradition has been for some authority outside the local congregation to make clergy appointments to specific posts. In the Roman Catholic Church this authority was usually the bishop, in some cases acting on the advice of his staff. In many cases, especially in Europe in the Middle Ages, church posts were under the authority of secular princes. Getting those appointments back under church authority has been an age-long battle. While church history has been enriched by tales such as the time the people of Milan chose Ambrose as their bishop by popular demand, in practice Catholic parishes have had relatively little to say in the selection and supervision of their own clergy. Modern Catholic reformers such as Schillebeeckx argue against this practice on New Testament grounds.[6] Yet despite such protests and the democratizing impulses of Vatican II, appointment remains hierarchically controlled.

In the Church of England today it is assumed that the parish will be consulted as to the kind of person needed and included in the discussion of specific names. Yet, because of the state-church character of Anglicanism, the power of appointment often still rests with a patron outside the Church. The bishop may have only nominal approval rights, and the wishes of the congregation may in fact be ignored. Obviously, this sort of system militates against any extensive consultation between the minister and those with whom he or she will be working.

The most that exists in these settings is not substantially different from the understanding I and my first congregation had in common, a kind of cultural norm. Anthony Russell's *The Clerical Profession* sets forth, for example, the traditional tasks of the Church of England minister.[7]

His chapter headings constitute the elements of the task: leader of public worship, preacher, celebrant of the sacraments, pastor, catechist, clerk, officer of law and order, almoner, teacher, officer of health, politician. Russell admits that many of these functions in many parishes have changed or disappeared over the years, but seems to assume that each incumbent will simply have to work out specific details in practice.

In the United States, with the exception of the Roman Catholic and United Methodist churches, the norm is for a congregational search committee to seek and sort nominations and to recommend, with varying degrees of finality, a candidate to the church. The central offices and governing bodies of the different denominations vary in the amount of structure and help they offer in the search process.

In Methodism, the bishop still appoints, but congregations have gained more say in the appointment process as the years have gone by. In Presbyterian life, the denomination ordains according to fairly strict standards and maintains a national placement office. The local presbytery must approve any ministers seeking work within its territory. There are suggested compensation guidelines for various levels of ministry, but the local congregation still chooses and negotiates with its own ministers.

Southern Baptists leave ordination and selection entirely to local congregations with only fragmentary placement systems operating in some state conventions and seminaries. In churches with the most active denominational participation, as in those with the broadest congregational authority, the norm still seems to be to expect that the minister as an ordained professional will know what he or she is to do. Salary and benefits are often, uncomfortably, negotiated, but very often little else is specified, and I have been able to discern no commonly accepted norm for establishing a ministerial contract.

In one sense, of course, given the varying traditions, the different sizes and financial resources of congregations, and the presence or absence of multiple-person staffs, no such norm is possible. At this point we can ask, "Are there pointers in scripture and theology or in secular professional practice to help us toward a contractual norm for ministers?"

Does the Bible offer any
help in negotiating a ministerial contract?

In many ways, the prevailing *ad hoc* pattern for establishing ministerial relationships is not substantially different from the rather fragmented and cryptic help we get from the New Testament. Churches and ministers have often relied on Paul's ostensible instructions to Timothy for the latter's ministry in Ephesus, with little or no critical attempt to adapt those instructions for other times and circumstances. Timothy, Paul said, should engage in the tasks of preaching, teaching, leadership, pastoral care, leading public worship, administration, and church discipline (1 Tim 4–5; 2 Tim 4:2-5). Paul's instructions, however, were intended for a particular minister in a specific situation in the context of imminent eschatological expectations.

There is no evidence that Paul intended his instructions to be seen as complete and comprehensive rather than suggestive. Nor, indeed, is there persuasive evidence the ministry in the modern professional sense had even been conceived of when Paul wrote. For example, in his work *Pastoral Ethics*, Gaylord Noyce suggests some texts that may have bearing on negotiating a minister's financial package, but then he downplays their applicability.[8] All we can do, then, is look for general principles for the conduct of ministers and extrapolate from them to a contractual relationship.

Paul's instructions to Timothy give us the generally accepted description of the character we expect a minister to display. These are the kinds of tests of character ordinands must meet even today in virtually every tradition. Churches in general expect the minister to conform to their particular interpretation of what these criteria mean. My little congregation in Kentucky had a finely-honed sense of what was proper conduct for me (and my spouse!) and what was not. Our tradition eschews alcohol. That particular congregation's covenant requires abstinence. They would have considered drinking even in moderation as grounds for dismissal.

The point to be taken here is no minister can function effectively who does not know and heed the cultural definitions of piety to which his or her congregation adheres. Nor is it possible without much time and great pain to alter those definitions. Normally they will not think their definitions wrong if you fail to conform. They will only think less of you.

Paul's injunction to women to be silent in the church at Corinth may have been given, for example, because the only women in Corinth who were not silent in public were the temple prostitutes. Similarly, Paul's awareness of cultural values and expectations at Ephesus seems to be behind his counsel to Timothy on how to relate to the various age and gender groups in the church. And the tone of his instructions to

Titus is unmistakably set by his belief that "Cretans are always liars, vicious brutes, lazy gluttons" (Titus 1:12).

Ministry must always take place within the context of the specific situation. Noyce even argues that ministers may occasionally have to accept congregational decisions they believe to be wrong for the sake of the overall ministerial relationship.[9] In entering into a ministerial situation, ministers must first be willing not only to place themselves under the discipline of a relationship to Christ but also to accept the discipline of maintaining a relationship of trust with a specific group of people. Divorce may be the only appropriate solution to a particular minister's marital problems, but in many churches that very solution will invalidate the congregation's trust in that same minister's leadership.

With regard to finances, the New Testament suggests two general principles that may be helpful in negotiating a salary package with a congregation. On the one hand, "the laborer is worthy of his hire." Paul spends much of 1 Corinthians 9 arguing that we in the ministry have a right to expect to make a decent living. "The Lord commanded that those who proclaim the gospel should get their living by the gospel" (v. 14). If not all churches have required a vow of poverty as in Roman Catholicism, still many have in effect said to the Lord of their minister, "You keep him humble, and we will keep him poor!" I see no scriptural reason for any minister to expect to make less than the average of the congregation he or she serves.

On the other hand, ministers should be careful to avoid any attempt to profit unduly from ministry. Regarding the need for ministerial submission to the Spirit of Christ when it comes to wages, Noyce points particularly to 1 Timothy 6:6-10.

> There is great gain in godliness combined with contentment; for we brought nothing into the world, so that we can take nothing out of it; but if we have food and clothing, we will be content with these. But those who want to be rich fall into temptation and are trapped by many senseless and harmful desires that plunge people into ruin and destruction. For the love of money is a root of all kinds of evil, and in their eagerness to be rich some have wandered away from the faith and pierced themselves with many pains.

We would have to look a long way to find a better description of the ultimately disastrous ambitions of some television ministers in recent years.

Still those of us whose ministries are in the normal range have to ask ourselves how we tell the difference between asking for too much and asking for enough to take adequate care of ourselves and our families. Perhaps what Paul suggests here is that those of us in the ministry should seek compensation at the level of sufficiency. We deserve enough to feed, clothe, and house our families; to provide them with adequate education, regular holidays, and adequate medical care; and to provide ourselves with a comfortable retirement. The New Testament definition of poverty is to lack enough for today. The New Testament definition of riches is to have more than enough. Ministers of Christ should be willing to live with enough. But they should undertake ministry at a financial sacrifice only if they and their families are willing to do so. When the Scripture says "He who does not take care of his own family is worse than an unbeliever," too many of us ministers seem to have skipped the page.

Beyond the principles of maturity in Christ, a willingness to work within the parameters of a specific situation, and monetary sufficiency, the New Testament offers little specific help for the minister as such. A few other more general scriptural principles are, however, worth mentioning. The commandment for adequate rest and worship applies to the pastor as much as to others. The teachings on spiritual gifts suggest that ministers should always seek to be honest with a congregation about what they can or cannot do. The same honesty, integrity, and forthrightness we expect of business people should be characteristic of the business aspects of our own profession.

Obviously, we end our scriptural survey where we began it. Scriptural principles are suggestive, but they cannot and indeed were never intended to give us a comprehensive program for establishing an effective ministerial relationship with a church. Rather, with scripture as a base, each of us must shape our own ministerial contract.

What are the elements in a Christian ministerial/congregational contract today?

In effect, what should I have asked and asked for, what should I have insisted on when the representatives of my Kentucky congregation and I first sat down to talk? More to the point, what should you insist on next time you enter negotiations with a church?

First, you should insist on full disclosure. When you enter negotiations with a church of your own denominational tradition, certain things will be assumed. It will be assumed that you are more or less doctrinally compatible, that you have similar views on salvation and ordination and the purpose and function of the church. For the most part, those externals will be fairly obvious. You probably won't talk seriously with any congregation whose stated views and traditions differ obviously from yours. If you work within a tradition in which clergy are assigned, few superiors would place you deliberately in a setting with which you are clearly incompatible.

Beyond the obvious, however, are all kinds of hidden factors that may affect your relationship. What is the congregation's immediate history? Why did the last minister in your position leave? What did the church like or dislike about him or her? Who are the power brokers within the congregation? Who are the disaffected? Is there some recent trauma or upcoming challenge concerning which they are reluctant to speak? How are decisions made and carried out both formally and informally? What expectations are there regarding your family? Does the church expect a certain style of leadership from you? Does the church leadership see the church as growing, stable, or declining during the next five years? What do they want to do?

Either in your discussions with the pastor search committee or in conversation with the whole church, you should insist on complete (if not necessarily satisfactory) answers to all questions about which you have any doubt. And you should be as honest with them as you are able to be about any questions they ask you. Interviewing for a ministry position is in one sense a job interview. In another sense, it is a corporate search for the will of God. As ministerial candidates, we must be less concerned about "looking good" than we are about seeking God's leadership. Be we ever so hungry, we must be less concerned about winning a job than about seeking the Lord's will.

In the interview process for the second pastorate I held, both my wife and I over the course of a weekend went through two extended question-and-answer sessions with the entire congregation. (She participated voluntarily, seeing herself as my ministry partner—as did I.) Their questions told us as much about them as our answers told them about us. The experience turned out quite happily. On the other hand in a similar experience with pulpit committee representatives of a large, wealthy church whose pastoral salary, at least, I would have liked to have, we quickly discovered we were socially incompatible with the congregation power brokers. Had we molded our presentation of ourselves in order to "get the job," everybody concerned would quickly have become miserable. Insist on full disclosure. Insist on it from the church you consider. Insist on it from yourself.

Second, before you agree to accept any position, develop and agree on a written job description. This process is often especially difficult for pastors, whose jobs tend to be thought of largely in traditional, nonspecific terms. "A pastor does what a pastor does." But if you are to be the pastor, the question is, "What will you do?" I was astounded the first time a pastor friend from another denomination told me his agreement with his church stated that he would work two evenings a week and no more. I thought of my own sense of guilt at the time when I worked less than four or five evenings and realized how much happier an experience he must be having than I. The fact I wish to emphasize here (although these days I set three evenings a week outside the home as a tentative personal maximum) is that a preexisting agreement eliminates guilt on the part of the minister. "I'm just not doing what I should be doing!" It also guards against unrealistic expectations on the part of the church. "Why doesn't this pastor visit on Thursday nights like the last one?"

Obviously, the nature of the pastorate is such that you must be available when others are at leisure and in crisis. Therefore, it is difficult to set a specific limit of workhours in a week. And, even if you have worked your allotted time, when someone dies you must go. Still it is possible to set a goal for a normal work week and to pursue that goal. It is enormously helpful to have some such periodic or hourly expectation built into the minister's contract. Nor should the minister be held to a biblical norm of six days' work if the rest of the congregation expects to work only five days.

Whatever the position, the job description should specify duties and expectations, work periods, vacations, benefits, and salary. And you should ask for what you want at the very begin ning. John Sanford argues this is critical in reducing ministerial burnout, even—with tongue not entirely in cheek—quoting Machiavelli, "If in order to achieve power you have to commit atrocities, it is better to commit them all at the very beginning."[10]

Your agreement should also include some clear pattern of accountability and method for performance feedback and evaluation. Bluntly, if you "screw up," they need a way to tell you; and if you have a complaint, you need a place to take it. To agree in advance on what those mechanisms will be is far better than trying to create them once a problem already exists. In general, within the framework of the ministry's peculiar nature, a written ministerial contract should include every provision necessary to give the minister a clear and detailed idea of what the church expects and will provide and to give the church a clear idea of what it may expect from the minister. This contract should then be reviewed regularly to permit adjustment and remind all parties of its provisions.

In addition, many ministers have found it helpful to begin their tenure with a special installation or covenant service. In this service both the minister and the congregation affirm their duties to one another by means of reciting a brief written covenant document. This covenant may then be repeated once a year. The congregation that has promised in worship to provide their minister with "time for study and reflection and family life" is much more likely to remember to do so than the congregation that never publicly acknowledges this obligation.

Third, above all, talk about and specify salary and benefits. Scripture is probably most explicit about this area of ministerial relations because this area has always given the church the greatest trouble. Scriptural investigation makes clear that the Bible nowhere suggests we ministers should deprive ourselves and our families of reasonable compensation. I suggested earlier that total compensation should be near the average for the congregation as a whole. Because ministers are considered self-employed, it is vital to specify who pays social security, pension fund, and medical benefits. Normal ministerial expenses such as housing, library, and travel should be considered. Financially, a ministerial contract should be every bit as complete and specific as that of any secular professional.

In negotiation with one congregation, I congratulated myself on having all financial matters specified and written down in advance. At the same time, I accepted a verbal assurance from the pastor search committee that they would "help us with a down payment," or co-invest, when the time came to buy a house. We arrived. The story changed, and only the intervention of a powerful church member from outside the committee assured that the promise was kept.

Fourth, there comes a point in contractual negotiation for a ministerial position at which you must get beyond the somewhat hard-nosed and cynical approach I have taken to this point. I have been concerned to inject some common sense into what traditionally has been a far-too-sloppy and inauthentically pious a process. Having done that, we must remember that for most churches and most believers choosing a new minister remains a somewhat mystical event. Beyond the contract there must be an affirmation of the common faith that makes the contract meaningful.

Here again, we can see the usefulness of a covenant between minister and congregation. The covenant could set out in simple terms an affirmation of your common faith, the parameters of your mutual duties, and the congregation's pledge of support to you as you undertake the ministry. The covenant thus puts the contractual process into the proper context of service to Christ and to his church. It reminds both parties that a ministerial contract is far more than an agreement between an employer and an employee. It is a mutual promise made in the presence of Almighty God.

Perhaps, you see, you will buy my argument and set out to secure a full, specific, written contract in advance of entering a ministerial position. But the question remains, "Will you then have guaranteed a sound ministerial relationship with the church?" The answer is "No." You will merely have cleared the way for such a relationship to be built. Ministry is mostly intangible. It takes place on the basis of trust and acceptance built over time. As such, it must be treated as more than contractual. Once you have planted the seed of servanthood and hedged it about against the predators that might steal the seed or chew up the young plant, you still must do the cultivation. Therefore, in the third section of this chapter we turn to the nitty gritty of ministry. How do we get things done? What are the ethics of leadership?

How can I build leadership in an ongoing relationship?

Suddenly you realize everyone in the room is looking at you. They're waiting for you to say what you think. This building committee has been working for months. They have kicked the issue around till if issues could show bruises, this one would be black and blue. And now it has come down to the critical moment. Does the church go ahead with this building project or not? And now they want to know what you think they should do. You are the servant of the church. You know your place as minister is not to dominate the will of the whole. Yet you are also the shepherd of the church, the one responsible for seeing the whole picture. Sometimes spiritual leadership is practical leadership. Sometimes practical decisions have tremendous spiritual implications. Tonight, if you do not lead, no one will. Your thoughts haven't taken more than a moment. Yet you realize the silence has grown expectant. It's time to get on with it. You open your mouth and begin to speak.

Perhaps nothing is more difficult for conscientious ministers than knowing how to work out their role in terms of the day-to-day leadership needs of the church. To say and do too much is to dominate. To say and do too little is to allow the church to drift. Ministers who know that their proper position within the church is one of servanthood also know that the writer of Proverbs said, "Where there is no vision, the people perish" (KJV). The minister who is much of a Hebrew scholar knows the literal translation of that verse: "Where there is no leader, the people break loose." And the minister intensely committed to a particular congregation's service very likely has a powerful sense of what that congregation's direction of movement ought to be. The question is, "How, ethically, how, practically, do you lead?" To get at an answer, we look first at leadership models as they have been brought to us through church tradition.

What are the basic historical models for church leadership?

If the question of the minister's authority is a theological issue, the problem of the minister's leadership style may be seen as the practical side of that same issue. The same basic divisions we saw when we looked at the hierarchical versus the non-hierarchical approaches to ministerial authority are present once again. It requires only a slight turn of the kaleidoscope for the pattern to fall into place from this new perspective.

In beginning, of course, the church drew its leadership models at least in part from Old Testament approaches adapted to the new situation of the church. The minister was a priest, yet not exactly a temple priest. The minister was a prophet, but more than a prophet. The minister was called and led by the Holy Spirit, but came to be seen as a kind of functionary. The minister was a teacher in the rabbinic sense, yet did more than a rabbi did. Add to these models the most prominent New Testament images—servant, shepherd, overseer, disciple, sinner—and you begin to get an idea of the rich primordial soup out of which the ministry emerged.

Perhaps the two greatest streams in the tradition were the need for organization and the impulse of the Spirit. Like hierarchicalism and the Protestant impulse, these two streams existed in tension. Catholicism sought to solve this tension by channeling spiritual legitimacy through the office of the priesthood itself. The result was leadership justified by office. Called by the Holy Spirit to a priestly vocation, the clergyman held the right to leadership by virtue of training, the assignment of responsibility by a superior in the hierarchy, and the spiritual legitimacy that came through ordination. To the extent that Christendom was a well-organized, systematic whole, and that those who found their way into the clergy were sincere, serious Christians, the system worked well. When clergy appointments were controlled by forces outside the church or based on criteria other than spiritual, the system broke down. Holding office was no guarantee that spiritual leadership was always present.

Still, both within the church hierarchy and outside it, the second stream, leaders by *charismata*, the gifts of the Spirit, have always been present. By reason of personal devotion and strength of personality, these were seen to have been gifted with the ability to lead. Very often they held office within the church; but, instead of deriving their right to lead from their office, their office drew its power from their personal gifts. When the people of Milan proclaimed Ambrose their bishop, they did so because of the gifts he already possessed. Martin Luther held no office in the hierarchy whatsoever when he became leader of the Reformation.

Such a brief sketch of 1500 years' history is obviously and admittedly oversimplified. Yet the truth is the church has given relatively little systematic attention to the problems of how to lead a congregation wisely and well. Christendom before the Reformation expected simple obedience to the church because the church was seen as the only legitimate channel for the Spirit into people's lives. Roman Catholicism till Vatican II continued in much the same vein, and, after those few heady years in the 1960s, the conservatives within that communion largely regained control. As a result, leadership by office is the dominant theme in Catholicism even today.

Protestantism's emphasis on the spiritual responsibility of the individual before God broke once and for all the dependence upon office as the necessary criterion for leadership. The Reformers emphasized spiritual gifts in a new way, seeing them not so much as bestowed at ordination but rather as necessary preconditions for ordination. The pastor, by holy life, example, diligent service, and devotion to spreading the gospel of salvation through Jesus, earned the right to speak and to be heard and heeded by the congregation. John Calvin wrote,

> They are mistaken if they suppose that Timothy so reigned in Ephesus and Titus in Crete as to dispose of all things at their own pleasure. They presided only by previously giving good and salutary counsels to the people.[11]

The history of Protestantism, of course, has been just as checkered as that of Catholicism in terms of the quality of leaders produced. Placing the leadership emphasis on the gifts of the individual opened the way for spiritual charlatanism of an entrepreneurial sort. The proliferation of sects and heresies comes at least in part from this individualistic emphasis. Anyone who can rent a hall and gather an audience becomes a spiritual leader in the eyes of some.

The second half of the twentieth century, and its emphasis on effectiveness in church growth has seen increasing attempts, especially among evangelicals, to borrow business models so as to inject efficiency and energy into the church's work. Peter Drucker's "management by objective" concept, for example, was for a time accepted almost whole cloth and put to use by clergy desperate for effective ways of getting things done in the local congregation. Today clergy desks are inundated by fliers advertising various business-model management techniques and the (costly) seminars that teach them. Each promises new growth and vitality for the church. Each suggests that leadership is neither a right of office nor a gift of the Spirit. It is rather a technique that can be learned and applied quite apart from spiritual values.

Those of us in the ministry thus find ourselves with much the same dilemma with regard to leadership that we face with regard to authority. Society is changing. The church is changing. Accepted historical models seem less than adequate now. Our own adoption of the servant model with respect to ministerial authority may be argued to leave us without the option of aggressive ministerial leadership in the daily life of the modern church. Can scripture help us once again?

Is there a practical biblical model for the nature of ministerial leadership in the church?

Obviously, the concepts of ministerial leadership and of authority within the church are in some ways inextricably intertwined. In the sketch with which we began this section, the minister had to decide how to exercise leadership in a building committee meeting. The ethical problem in part is that some ministers in some congregations carry so much authority, their opinion would have the force of law. (That's never been a problem in churches I've served, but perhaps it has been for you!) So how do ministers maintain what we have seen as an ethically correct posture of servanthood and fulfill their responsibility to lead the church?

The biblical answer, I believe, is found in a further exploration of New Testament concepts of ministry. If servanthood is seen as the basis for ministerial authority, it is also the touchstone from which leadership develops. Yet there is another dimension to servanthood beyond that of acting as a servant of the church. Paul said to the church at Corinth, "Think of us in this way, as servants of Christ and stewards of God's mysteries" (1 Cor 4:1). There is an element to ministerial servanthood that takes precedence over service to the church. That is service to God.

As stewards, ministers are responsible to God for the welfare of the church in their care. That responsibility provides the impetus to aggressive leadership that servanthood by itself is lacking. Jesus served the disciples but never let their opinions come between him and his duty to God as he perceived it. Often he went quietly on the way he believed he must follow regardless of what they said. Thomas and the others, for example, seem to have warned him that he was in danger if he went to Jerusalem. Still, he went ahead. To be a steward in the biblical sense is to hold responsibility for taking care of a treasure while the owner is away. Ministers find themselves in exactly that position in Christ's church.

Similarly, in the image of pastor/shepherd we find a responsibility for spiritual and physical oversight of the flock. The term *episkopos,* which the hierarchical churches translate as bishop and the free churches interpret as pastor, means, literally, the overseer. Clearly, then, serving as a pastor is in one sense taking responsibility for the whole welfare of the church. It involves an administrative role in some ways analogous to that of a CEO (chief executive officer) in corporate life, but perhaps in more ways analogous to that of a foreman or departmental supervisor. The pastor, in fact, never properly operates on his or her own authority but rather in the context of the larger responsibility to Christ that characterizes the church as a whole.

Neither Paul nor any of the other New Testament leaders ever hesitated to state their opinions or exert their influence in an attempt to move the church in the way they thought it should go. Indeed, it could be argued that the whole of the Epistles consists precisely of examples of various means of pastoral leadership–teaching, preaching, encouragement, admonition, and personal opinion.

Sometimes in the New Testament pastoral leadership required a firm hand. Again and again, Jesus confronted sin by calling it what it was, in no uncertain terms. When Paul wrote to the church at Galatia, he called them "foolish" for abandoning grace in favor of a return to legalism. His first letter to the Corinthians is a model of pastoral sorrow and moral indignation: "It is actually reported that there is sexual immorality among you!" Yet there are also examples of a much lighter touch. The note to Philemon about his runaway slave Onesimus is a classic in the gentle art of pastoral persuasion. Jesus' reply to Herod, "Go tell that fox!" shows appreciation for Herod's cunning as well as an awareness of Herod's sin. The long interchange with the Samaritan woman at the well is a model of firm gentleness.

In sum, then, working out of Jesus' model of servanthood, with a firm personal commitment to Christ and an eye toward Christ's vision for the church, ministers act in each situation to move individuals and the church as a whole in the direction they believe Christ would have them go. Ministers do so in the full awareness that their own perception of Christ's leadership and of the situation in which they work may be flawed. The minister's advocacy is never undertaken in arrogance but always in humility. Servanthood, stewardship, pastoral care, and oversight are thus held in balance and engender the creative tension within which the minister lives and works. Of course, all of this sounds very nice, but we are left with the more practical question, "Can this New Testament ideal for ministerial leadership actually be made to work within late twentieth-century church life?"

How does one live out
a biblical ministerial leadership model today?

From the discussion above we can derive at least three principles that should inform the leadership decisions we as ministers must make.

First, the minister leads as a servant of the church. Ministry is never from above; ministry is always from below. Or perhaps, as Gaylord Noyce suggests, the best way to talk about this is as ministry from within.[12] When we commit ourselves to a congregation, we become, as Jesus styled his disciples, "friends," or as Paul talked about himself with regard to the Philippians, "fellow laborers" with them in the work of the gospel. While we expect our servanthood to be of a type that earns us influence and the right to leadership in decision-making, we also, as part of our commitment, accept that they are seeking Christ's leadership too, and that their perceptions may in fact be keener than our own.

What exactly, then, would we expect our minister in the building committee meeting to say? We would expect her to give her best evaluation of the situation as a whole, to set her opinion in the context of her personal understanding of the mission of that congregation and, at the same time, to leave room for others in the congregation to disagree. Servants must always stand ready for correction from those whom they serve. We are servants of the church.

Second, though, and more important, we are servants of the Lord. Our eyes are to be focused on the Christ we follow. In our discussion of ministerial authority we dealt with Luther's point that the minister's authority is always based on faithfulness to the gospel, by which he meant spreading the good news of salvation by grace through faith in Jesus Christ. Each tradition is likely to state a little differently this essential element of following Christ. Clearly, though, the minister's responsibility is to keep focused on Christ, and to keep the people focused on Christ, to help them if they lack understanding and to point them back toward Christ if they stray.

You might find yourself in a building committee meeting in which you believed strongly that the committee should vote to go ahead with the project. You might believe that going forward was an act of faith in Christ the church needed desperately to take, and that failing to go forward would be to deny the very ministry to which Christ had called the church. If so, allowing for the specific dynamics of the personalities, your role would be to speak strongly to that point–Christ's call for this church and how this project will answer that call.

The corollary question, of course, is "What if you lose?" You speak as strongly as you can, and the church chooses to ignore your leadership and go in another direction. Then what?

This leads us to the third principle. The point of leadership is the welfare of the church, "building up the body of Christ for the work of the ministry," as Paul said in Ephesians. Very often in ministry we will find that we have a clear sense of where the church needs to go, but the church will not be ready to follow. The members may be frightened of change. They may be discouraged by previous failure. They may not see their ministry in the same direction we do.

Our own ideas may be wrong, or we may not yet have earned the right of leadership by sufficient service. The key at such times is to remember the purpose of leadership. If that purpose is the welfare of Christ's church, then leadership may involve slowing down, accepting defeat on an issue now in the interest of building a relationship that will let you move forward later. It may involve going back to the basics of discipling, communicating your vision in more individual ways. The work of the ministry, after all, is their work. Noyce says that may even mean accepting with good grace a decision you know to be wrong.

Of course, if the church moves strongly in a direction that infringes on your conscience, you do have one other weapon for bringing them around. You can confront, with a view to resignation. Be advised, however, that in such a case you will almost certainly need to go ahead and resign. And remember, as a wise pastor once told me, "Before you crawl up on a cross, be at least reasonably certain it is for the salvation of the world."

The final principle, implicit in the other three and explicit in the nature of the overseer, is that leadership is active. The secular view and the view of certain brands of piety is that the ministry is essentially a passive occupation. You sit in your study and wait for people to bring their problems to you. You move from one priestly task to another in a kind of holy haze. Nothing could be further from the truth. The overseer pays constant attention to a thousand details, bringing each into harmony with the overall purpose of the church. Like a sculptor, he or she chips away at everything not in harmony with the grand design. The leader is passionately involved in shaping the direction of the church's life.

On our building committee an active minister would have been involved in forming and defining the task of the committee in the first place. The minister would know the leanings of the committee members. She would have kept enough abreast of the committee's work to have formed a good opinion of the project's practicability and of the committee's inclination either to go ahead or not. An active ministerial leader would not come to the moment of truth and need to ask himself what to give as a word of pastoral leadership. Without manipulation, respecting the integrity of the process, he would have done his homework all the way along. He would know what to say and they would say it confidently and clearly.

Ministerial leadership, of course, is expressed in a myriad of ways in the minister's daily life and work. At each point we encounter the same kind of dilemma. How do I preach so as to honor God, communicate the gospel, and not abuse the congrega tion's intellect or emotions? Do I teach them to think like I think or to think for themselves? What are the ethical parameters of pastoral counseling? Chapter 5 will explore this next set of ethical issues in ministry.

Notes

[1]Bernard Ramm, *The Pattern of Religious Authority* (Grand Rapids MI: Eerdmans, 1959) 10.

[2]*Annual of the Southern Baptist Convention,* 1988, 69.

[3]Gert Haendlen, *Luther on Ministerial Office and Congregational Function* (Philadelphia: Fortress, 1981) 30f, 56f.

[4]Hans Kung, *The Church,* trans. Ray and Rosaleen Ockenden (New York: Sheed and Ward, 1968) 392.

[5]Karl Barth, *Church Dogmatics,* IV 2, 690-91.

[6]Hans Schillebeeckx in *The Teaching Authority of the Believer,* Metz and Schillebeeckx, eds. (Edinburgh: T. & T. Clark, 1985) 17ff.

[7]Anthony Russell, *The Clerical Profession* (London: SPCK, 1980).

[8]Gaylord Noyce, *Pastoral Ethics* (Nashville: Abingdon, 1988) 113-18.

[9]Noyce, 46.

[10]John A. Sanford, *Ministerial Burnout* (London: Arthur James Ltd., 1987) 35.

[11]John Calvin, *Institutes of the Christian Religion,* IV, iii, 15.

[12]Noyce, 32.

CHAPTER 5

SHEPHERDING

Now we come to the central functions of the ministerial life: preaching, teaching, and pastoral care. These are the shepherding functions. All ministers will spend much of their working life in direct contact with people in one of these three ways. In each of them ministers will face significant opportunities for shaping the spiritual and moral lives of their people.

We will reserve our last chapter for the challenging ethical considerations of the prophetic function. In this chapter we seek to focus on the normal life of the minister. There is not space, of course, for anything approaching a full treatment of the ethical issues involved in these three functions. Rather the attempt will be to focus suggestively on the kinds of issues that may arise in the normal course of ministerial practice, in the hope that the principles derived will point the way for dealing with new problems as they appear.

How do I preach ethically as a Christian?

It was late Thursday afternoon, sermon day. But John had written very little so far. He got up from his desk and headed for the fifth cup of coffee of the afternoon, wondering if his digestion would survive the outrage. Concentration was so far gone, though, he did not even make it across the room. The view out his study window caught his eye: the shabby lawn, the children's playground in sad need of renovation, the church façade showing the deterioration of years of neglect. Ten minutes later he was still standing there.

He knew what the problem was. His denomination's tradition was for confrontational, challenging, demanding preaching. It had taken him years to get past the guilt that kind of preaching produced in him. His own ministry had been spent in large measure in reaction against that tradition. His sermons tended to major on grace, healing, and reconciliation. People loved his sermons.

But lately he had begun wondering if he was wrong. Giving was down. The Sunday School organization was in a shambles for lack of workers. There were fewer new members than there had been in five years. "I wonder," he mused for the thousandth time that day. "I wonder if I've been doing it wrong. I've always believed Jesus' message was the message of grace. I hate preaching for guilt. I hate manipulating anybody. But for all my grace, nobody's responding! Would it be wrong to be more demanding? What if I told a few tear-jerkers? Could I stand it? What should I do?"

What is the history of the ethics of preaching as a practice within the Christian church?

Preaching, of course, has always been at the heart of the Christian faith—so much so that for most of us within the church, the ethics of preaching will forever be the ethics of preaching as we have heard and experienced it within our own faith community. One must therefore admit at the outset that what is said in these pages will be sharply colored by the cultural context within which these observations are heard.

The average sermon in a mainline university congregation in a large city will be radically different in form, content, and presentation than that in a small rural church. The Catholic and Protestant sermons in a given community on a given day may differ substantially from each other as will those given in blue and white collar congregations or in congregations of differing ethnic backgrounds. Nor is it our purpose in this section to provide a description of how to preach, but rather to suggest the most common ethical considerations that preachers of all traditions must encounter and deal with.

Having said that, we are free to ask what is the history of ethical considerations in preaching. Raymond Bailey points out that at least as early as the prophet Jeremiah (23:20), preachers were stealing one another's material.[1] So plagiarism has always been with us. So have preaching from self-interest (the prophets of Baal who contended with Elijah) and preaching a lie (ditto). So also has the practice of a preacher taking credit for what God has done (Moses striking the rock with his stick instead of calling forth water at the command of God). In the New Testament those who knew not Jesus cast out demons in his name, and Paul in Acts reprimands Peter for failing to practice what he preached with regard to welcoming gentiles into the church.

With the church fathers and the organization of Christendom into congregations, preaching began its process of development into a high art. By the fourth century we can identify a number of prominent practitioners. John Chrysostom, who preached in Antioch, pointed out how the life of the minister is judged by the parish on the standards of angels rather than ordinary mortals. Any moral failure is likely to bring condemnation.[2]

Ambrose, who was so popular with the people of Milan that they elevated him to bishop over his strongest objections, defended the prophetic function of the preacher, with which we will deal in our final chapter. In a letter to Theodosius, Ambrose argued, "There is nothing in a priest so full of peril as regards God or so base in the opinion of men, as not freely to declare what he thinks."[3] Pulpit freedom has been a consistent ethical goal through much of Christian history. It has also been consistently endangered and challenged.

Augustine is remembered as a consummate preacher. A chief ethical argument of his regarded the necessity of the pastor staying with his church in time of persecution. George H. Williams observed,

> The most vivid aspect of the *Vita* is its preservation of Augustine's own words concerning the self-sacrifice of the pastor in times of persecution or invasion(the Vandals). Herein he gives voice to what we might call the professional ethic of the clergyman (sic) who like the captain, must go down with his ship, or, like the shepherd, give his life for his flock; for ". . . the ties of our ministry, by which the love of Christ has bound us not to desert the churches . . . should not be broken."[4]

That principle of practicing what one preaches informed the central issue in the controversy over the Donatian heresy, though in that application Augustine opted for a sacramentalist position.

With the advent of the Middle Ages the church became the dominant power in the West. Its preaching, in contrast to the antiestablishment character of earlier times, became more and more the expression of the dominant culture, a means of socialization and control of the masses. Perhaps the best example of this is the radical shift in the content of preaching with regard to war and peace. In the change from the pacifism of Jesus to the holy war ethic of Urban II's call for the First Crusade, there is a millenial shift in far more than time. As preaching became the expression of the dominant culture rather than a protest against the dominant culture, impetus for the examination of the ethics of the methodology of preaching died out.

The result, I would argue, is that for most of church history the ethics of preaching has been a function of the particular cultural context in which the preaching event took place. Preachers have tended to support and affirm the ecclesiastical culture within which they found themselves. The essence of the Reformation was a preachers' protest against maintaining that cultural compulsion. But even in the Reformation the ethics of preaching itself were little examined. Martin Luther was quite capable of condemning his enemies from the pulpit in terms every bit as vicious as those they used against him.

The great contribution of the Reformation to preaching ethics is the reintroduction of the biblical touchstone as an authority for the content of preaching that is to some degree independent of cultural traditions. That authority, in Protestant circles at least, sets parameters for the kind of discourse that will be considered as Christian preaching in the broad sense. With the corollary principle of the soul competency of the individual in matters of religion, the Reformation thus provides a means by which preaching may be kept from some of its more abusive tendencies. Still little attention is paid in formal thought to the ethics of preaching itself.

Even today in theological education ethics and preaching are regarded as essentially separate disciplines—a matter of considerable humor, if one stops to think about it! While there was a good deal of talk during my own theological education in the 1970s about the ethics of manipulative preaching and of the new market-oriented methodologies of church growth that were just beginning to emerge, there was little or no formal discussion of the ethics of preaching itself. I cannot honestly recall even one full class period devoted to the subject. Raymond H. Bailey, longtime professor of preaching at the Southern Baptist Theological Seminary and a pastor himself, observes:

> Homiletics books allot little space to the ethics of sermon preparation and presentation. Perhaps this is because they assume the common standards of propriety for academics, politics, business, and literature with regard to respect for the audience, respect for the work of others, and respect for truth will prevail. . . . The homileticians devote far more attention to personal morality and piety than to pulpit integrity.[5]

The problem is those standards cannot now be assumed, if indeed they ever could. *Elmer Gantry* of the popular novel has become a fictional prototype for the real-life lack of integrity in pulpits today. The vast majority of preachers continue to be sincere servants of Christ who work hard to make their preaching reflective of their own experience. But there are enough documented instances of abuse to make the public increasingly cynical of the motives and methods of preaching today. Unethical preaching is as common as adultery in Christian life in the late twentieth century. One could argue it is at least as destructive.

What insight does scripture offer
regarding the ethics of preaching?

As with most of the subjects in this book, scripture is more engaged in the doing of preaching than it is in theorizing about it. Nonetheless, we can gain several insights. First, authentic preaching is done only at the call of God. The record suggests a reluctance on the part of many biblical preachers to say anything at all for public consumption except under compulsion of the Spirit. Moses spent the early part of Exodus (chaps. 3–4) arguing with God that he could not possibly be the best available candidate to speak on behalf of the Hebrews:

> O my Lord, I have never been eloquent, neither in the past nor even now that you have spoken to your servant; but I am slow of speech and slow of tongue. (4:10)

Only when God grew angry at his unwillingness did Moses relent and accede to act as God's spokesperson.

Isaiah, similarly, was struck reluctant by his own unworthiness at the call of God

> And I said, "Woe is me! For I am lost, for I am a man of unclean lips, and I live among a people of unclean lips; yet my eyes have seen the King, the Lord of Hosts." Then one of the seraphs flew to me, holding a live coal that had been taken from the altar with a pair of tongs. The seraph touched my mouth with it and said: "Now that this has touched your lips, your guilt has departed and your sin is blotted out." Then I heard the voice of the Lord saying, "Whom shall I send, and who will go for us?" And I said "Here am I; send me!" And he said "Go and say to this people." (6:5-9a)

Only when his sense of inadequacy was dealt with did Isaiah feel worthy of speaking to the people for God. The significant point is that authentic preaching, from a biblical point of view, *always* comes at the impetus of the Spirit.

In fairness, scripture does not appear to restrict preaching to the authorized version. On one occasion the disciples asked Jesus to denounce one, not of their number, who was casting out demons in the name of Jesus. Jesus refused, saying, "Whoever is not against us is for us" (Mark 9:40). Yet Jesus also cautioned against insincerity.

> On that day many will say to me "Lord, Lord, did we not prophecy in your name, and cast out demons in your name, and do many deeds of

power in your name?" Then I will declare to them, "I never knew you. Go away from me, you evildoers." (Matt 7:22-23)

Preaching, to be authentic, can only take place when the one preaching is in genuine fellowship with the Spirit of Christ.

The preacher must be careful to put Christ first in personal loyalty. John the Baptist was the greatest preacher of Jesus' generation. As Jesus' popularity grew, John's disciples confronted John with the inevitable conflict between their respective followers. John answered,

> The friend of the bridegroom, who stands and hears him, rejoices greatly at the bridegroom's voice. For this reason my joy has been fulfilled. He must increase, but I must decrease. (John 3:29b-30)

This particular text has often been used in Christian practice as the basis for ordination sermons. Ordinands are urged to commit themselves to a life of magnifying Christ rather than self.

A second Johannine text makes the same argument in the words of Jesus:

> Those who speak on their own seek their own glory; but the one who seeks the glory of him who sent him is true, and there is nothing false in him. (7:18)

Jesus was speaking of his own true representation of God. The application, however, holds true for those who would speak for Jesus as well. The words of Paul confirm the point:

> I did not come proclaiming the mystery of God to you in lofty words or wisdom. For I decided to know nothing among you except Jesus Christ, and him crucified. . . . My speech and my proclamation were not with plausible words of wisdom, but with a demonstration of the Spirit and of power. (1 Cor 2:1b-2, 4)

Ethical preaching, in the Christian tradition, must be Christocentric. There is no other way.

Paul's argument suggests a further application as well. Ethical preaching should avoid being elegantly manipulative. Techniques of persuasion and manipulation of audiences have become common currency in the 1990s. Every preacher likes to get a response, and, with many audiences, producing a particular response is simply a matter of applying certain persuasive techniques. Paul would abhor all such practices as foreign to the spirit and simplicity of Christ's message.

We have renounced disgraceful, underhanded ways; we refuse to practice cunning or to tamper with God's word, but by the open statement of the truth we would commend ourselves to the conscience of everyone in the sight of God. (2 Cor 4:2, author's rendering)

Jesus himself declined ever to make the commitment he asked for too easy to apprehend.

At the same time, ethical preaching is always intensely relevant to the specific life situation of the hearers. Jesus consistently tailored his messages to the situations of those to whom he spoke. Paul's sermon at the Areopagus in Athens put the gospel in terms the Athenians could understand. Again and again the apostles found ways to tell the story of Christ in new images for new hearers. There is nothing inherently wrong with using highly culturalized and specific techniques of portraying the gospel as long as no violence is done to the gospel message itself, to the integrity of transmission of that message, or to the freedom of its hearers to respond or not as they may choose.

The New Testament preachers never shirked dealing with difficult subjects because they would meet opposition or create dissent. They spoke, as Paul commanded, "the truth in love" (Eph 4:15). The elder's advice to Timothy speaks of that kind of determined, loving persistence:

I solemnly urge you: proclaim the message; be persistent whether the time is favorable or unfavorable; convince, rebuke, and encourage, with the utmost patience in teaching. (2 Tim 4:2-3)

Preaching in a parish situation must necessarily take a scattergun approach. Some will hear on a given day. Others will not be ready or will not be feeling well that day or will be distracted by the company coming to Sunday dinner. The essential gospel message must be presented Sunday after Sunday from a variety of perspectives so that it can be heard over time by the broadest possible section of the people.

What are the essential elements of a valid preaching ethic for today?

Two contemporary sources will serve as springboards for this section. Raymond Bailey's article in *Review and Expositor* lists and deals with six ethical problems related to preaching: plagiarism, poor preparation and faulty exegesis, glittering generalities, loaded language and name calling, emotional manipulation, misrepresentation and partial truth.[6] Gaylord Noyce lists five: (1) faithfulness to the true goal of preaching, (2) accountability in relation to scripture, (3) integrity in the way we use sources and in avoiding plagiarism, (4) respect for other participants—the congregation—in the "preaching event," and (5) "some affirmations and caution in preaching on social issues."[7]

John's problem in the vignette with which we began this section is the problem of how to use this incredible opportunity of preaching. Is its purpose to recruit converts, to edify believers, to build the church as an institution, to confront evil in the membership and in society, to comfort, to challenge, or some combination of all of these? And given that one can settle on a purpose for preaching, what are the ethically acceptable parameters that must characterize the preaching event itself? Both Bailey and Noyce make legitimate attempts to set those parameters. But it seems to me that a prior statement of the purpose of preaching will help to inform our discussion.

Briefly, authentic Christian preaching presents the gospel of Jesus Christ to audiences under the guidance of the Holy Spirit in such a way as to confront, challenge, convert, teach, comfort, elucidate, and exemplify its (the gospel's) true nature. Thus, preaching the gospel must be done in gospel fashion. Both its substance and form must be coherent with the values the gospel upholds.

Having said this, it becomes clear why some of the above cited elements of an ethic of preaching are important. A gospel presentation that talks about truth and honesty in conduct cannot be gospel unless it is honest in and of itself. Hence plagiarism, the use of others' work without proper credit, is unacceptable in the practice of preaching. Bailey particularly refers to the common practice of appropriating experiences or stories told by others and repackaging them as one's own. It is a simple matter to give credit for ideas or stories without detracting from the telling of them. One feels compelled to cite Jesus' admonition to "Let your word be 'Yes, Yes' or 'No, No'; anything more than this comes from the evil one" (Matt 5:37). Just like swearing falsely, plagiarizing stories makes what is not appear to be what is and is therefore unacceptable.

Fidelity to scripture is a second point we must deal with. The question, of course, is "What constitutes authentic fidelity to scripture in preaching?" Many denominations are torn in debate between those who favor a more "literal" interpretation of scripture and thus of scripture's authority for our lives and those who favor a less literal, more scholarly method of interpretation.

For purposes of ethical preaching, one's preaching should be consistent with one's theology. Preachers who espouse a literal interpretation of scripture owe it to their audience and to their Lord to apply that literalism consistently. Preachers who believe in the use of scholarly techniques of interpretation should not forgo those techniques simply because a more literal interpretation is convenient in a given instance. *Eisegesis*, reading into scripture what is not there simply because it happens to be convenient to one's desired sermon objective, remains one of the most common ethical problems in preaching across all theological divisions.

A small but crucial point is that scripture itself must never be violated in the preaching act. I once heard a famous preacher in my denomination read the text for the sermon he was about to present. Because I happened to be following the reading in my own Bible, I discovered that he was actually altering his reading of scripture to conform to the outline of the sermon he wished to preach! Even worse, at no time did he tell those of us in the congregation that he had done this. The proliferation of translations and paraphrases in recent years makes it essential that the preacher inform the congregation which translation is being used and how his or her own translation may differ. Otherwise there is no integrity of interpretation.

A third major element in the development of a consistent ethic of preaching is that the preacher must learn to distinguish between emotional appeal and emotional manipulation. That is not always easy to do. My wife and I once visited a congregation in which the choir began to hum in preparation for the altar call while the preacher was speaking his last few paragraphs. It sounds laughable in the telling. I am sure that preacher thought it a normal and appropriate technique, but in the context of that service it felt to us like manipulation, and we resented it.

We expect preaching to appeal both to our intellect and our emotions. Preaching that is devoid of emotional content leaves people bored and indifferent. Jesus could and did both give fiery denunciations of evildoers and tell stories that tugged at the heartstrings. The key seems to be that preaching should never seek by unfair manipulation of the emotions to produce a response that would be other than the freely considered choice of those listening.

By the same token, fourth, preaching must be intellectually honest. Bailey's talk about "glittering generalizations" and misrepresentation of the facts highlights this. Ministers are often unintentionally guilty of dishonesty by "dumbing down" their biblical interpretation to make it more palatable to theologically unsophisticated congregations. For example, a minister who has been taught and believes that Genesis 1 and 2 form a poetic rather than a literal account of the beginning of creation may find it easier to preach as though the stories are to be taken literally. That dishonesty both impedes engaging the text and hinders the growth in understanding of the congregation.

One would think it did not need to be said that the preacher must not lie or misrepresent facts to a congregation in the process of preaching. Actual practice in the United States shows otherwise, especially with the growth of the Religious Right in American politics. The political preachers of the Right have not hesitated to lie about their political enemies. When confronted they have tended to argue in the fashion of situation ethics that the end justifies the means. Bailey points out, however, that at least in some circles, the phrase "ministerially speaking" has become a common euphemism for exaggeration. That connotation appeared long before the Religious Right. It suggests that people at large expect their ministers to play fast and loose with the truth when it suits their purposes and hints at the pervasive ethical rot in American church life.

A positive way of summarizing the previous two points is that preaching must respect the integrity and freedom of choice of the listener. In presenting their version of the truth, preachers do so in such a way that listeners are appealed to without being coerced, intrigued without being intruded upon, challenged and confronted but never abused. The story is told that Jonathan Edwards, who helped spark America's Great Awakening, particularly with his oft-repeated sermon "Sinners in the Hands of an Angry God," used to preach that sermon in a monotone while staring at the bell rope in the back of the sanctuary. The sermon is a combination both of what is said and of how it is said. Either content or style may err in the direction of manipulation. Both content and style may be appealing, but neither should be unfair.

A fifth element in the ethics of preaching concerns the balance in overall presentation of the gospel to a specific congregation. The Roman church throughout its history and the mainline Protestant churches today generally follow a cycle of preaching designed to present the whole gospel story over a three-year cycle. Free church tradition has been much less intentional in its approach to the overall picture. Preaching that focuses only on evangelism or only on Christian nurture or only on contemporary issues or only on the institutional concerns of the congregation fails to present the richness and variety of the gospel message.

Preachers need to make an effort to vary the tone and subject matter of preaching so that over time the range of congregational needs and concerns are dealt with. Otherwise, the gospel is misrepresented. The Jesus who declared that "when the Spirit of truth comes, he will guide you into all the truth" (John 16:13a) could not have intended his followers to omit or shrink from any direction in which the Spirit leads.

Noyce points to a sixth area of concern in his search for a balance in presentation of social issues.

> The pastoral and the prophetic dimensions of ministry are intimately linked arguments to the contrary notwithstanding. The conscientious pastor cannot choose one and neglect the other. True pastoral caring knows human beings live in and derive moral meanings from their social environment. Concern for this environment is concern for persons.[8]

As my ethics professor Henlee Barnette used to say, "There is but one gospel, and it is both personal and social." Having said that, however, we will leave a fuller examination of this issue for the sixth chapter of this book. Suffice it to say that the minister must judge carefully when and how to focus on social issues as they arise in the context of a congregation's life. They must neither be ignored nor allowed to assume sole attention. On the one extreme lies social irresponsibility and irrelevance. On the other lies spiritual exhaustion.

Finally, preaching must be an honest reflection of the authentic spiritual life of the one preaching, without allowing the individual's personal problems to be visited on the congregation. Jesus, as we saw in our examination of the scripture, reserved some of his strongest condemnation for those who preached outside their own experience. Preaching must be "confessional" in the sense that it recognizes honestly the individual's struggles and doubts in the face of the issues of life. Preacher who will not admit their own struggle with mortality cannot help the congregation as they struggle with theirs. Inevitably, preaching will reflect the spiritual limitations and immaturities of the preacher. It is necessary to recognize that fact and to struggle to magnify Christ in the midst of one's own limitations.

One of the least ethical things preachers can do is to "take out" their own anger or frustration on an unsuspecting congregation. At the most basic level, preaching is bound by the admonition of *agape,* love that wills and works for the well-being of the other. For the sake of the well-being of the congregation, preachers need to be careful to work on their own spiritual issues somewhere other than in the pulpit. They need to work constantly to be aware of where they are in their own personality and relationship to Christ, and to maintain enough objectivity to recognize when personal issues are impeding the presentation and purity of the gospel message.

What ethical guidelines apply for my service as a teacher?

For the first time, Ted found his steps slowing as he headed across campus for his Thursday afternoon discipleship group at University Church. A thoughtful student, he had invested a lot of energy working on faith issues during his time in college. Now, in his junior year, he had begun to move toward a sense of reconciliation between the simple faith of his childhood and a more reasoned, adult approach. He had started asking questions he had never dared ask before. In recent weeks, he'd even found courage to challenge some of the dogmatism of his charismatic, conservative pastor, Rev. Mack.

Things had come to a kind of head the week before in the regular Thursday afternoon study group Rev. Mack led for university men. Actually that was the issue. There were no discipleship groups at the church for university women, despite the huge student population, and, when Ted asked why, Rev. Mack first tried to brush off the question. Then, when Ted persisted, he took refuge in pastoral authority.

"Now Ted, that's nothing for an engineering major to worry about! I've told you many times that Scripture teaches men are to be the spiritual leaders. Shouldn't you trust me?"

"I don't see why I can't ask the question," Ted had pursued. "A lot of people think the Bible supports women in ministry."

"Our denomination doesn't! And I don't! Isn't it spiritually arrogant to challenge your God-ordained leaders this way, Ted? Now, come on, let's get back to Revelation!"

Ted slowed to a stop and sat down on a bench there in the May sunshine. He realized he did not want to go back to discipleship group again! He felt abused by what pastor Mack had done, and he felt guilty for feeling abused. Either way it was awkward, and he did not want to put himself in that situation again. "I think I'll go to the Union, instead," he decided. "Maybe I can get up a game of pool."

How has the church dealt with the ethics of the teaching ministry?

On the one hand, the teaching ministry holds an ancient and honored place in the work of the church. As Paul said in First Corinthians 12:28, God has appointed first the apostles, "second prophets, third teachers." John Knox argued, however, that there was always an interrelatedness of both purpose and identity between the prophetic and teaching functions.

> The word "teacher" suggests instruction in the more ordinary sense, a setting forth, perhaps in somewhat more objective fashion of the facts of the tradition and the truth of the gospel, the inculcation of true beliefs, the encouraging of appropriate ethical impulses and conduct. The epistles of the New Testament show us the teacher at work. . . . But the line between prophet and teacher in the primitive church is not easy to draw: the prophet would often have been—indeed, how could he have helped being?—also the teacher; and the teacher would often have been the prophet. It is likely that since the more ecstatic endowment of the prophet would have seemed more exalted, the teacher who possessed it would usually have been called a prophet; but even he would have found it impossible to distinguish between his "prophecy" and his "teaching."[9]

In point of fact, the great teachers through much of church history have often also been the great preachers. It is hardly fair, for example, to argue that Martin Luther was not preaching in his pamphlets or teaching in his sermons. Indeed, he was doing both in both. Despite that interrelation and the consequent back seat that teaching has often taken to preaching, clear traditions of teaching may be discerned from the earliest days of the church.

In the earliest years, teaching had two primary functions in the church. First was the clarification of the true meaning of the gospel and the true way of Christian practice for those within the faith. The *Didache* suggests,

> XI. Whoever then shall come and teach you all the aforesaid, receive him. But if the teacher himself turn and teach another doctrine to destroy this, do not listen to him; but if it be to the increase of righteousness and of the knowledge of the Lord, receive him as the Lord

. . . . Every prophet that teacheth the truth, if he doeth not the things that he teacheth, is a false prophet.[10]

Reflecting the intensely practical character of the age, the writer was careful to suggest that a prophet who wanted to stay more than two or three days without working toward self-support was by definition a false prophet. Character and teaching had to be seen to be congruent before the churches were required to accept any teacher.

The second primary function of Christan teaching in the earliest years was to interpret and, it was hoped, legitimize the faith for those outside the church. Justin's *Apology* from about the year 150 was written to provide that kind of explanation for pagan readers. On the Christian practice of worshiping on Sunday, for example, he said,

We hold our common assembly on the day of the sun, because it is the first day, on which God put to flight darkness and chaos and made the world, and on the same day Jesus Christ our Savior rose from the dead.[11]

In apologetic work the emphasis was on clarity and appeal in description of the practices of the church, in order to refute the charges against them common in pagan society.

As the church grew more and more widespread, the dominant function of Christian teaching came to be to define and enforce orthodoxy for the church as a whole. Described here in a sentence, that process took centuries of writings, the promulgation of successive creeds and catechisms, and a number of councils. It is at least appropriate to say, however, that by the high Middle Ages, the chief function of teaching in the churches of the West was the inculcation and enforcement of Catholic orthodoxy. Both the later monastic orders and the universities that began to arise after the first millenium did so with that explicit charge, though they also became centers of innovation. Medieval scholasticism thus both codified the ancient faith and modified it considerably in the process.

The Dominicans, and later the Jesuits, were given particular responsibility for enforcing orthodoxy. The Inquisition, which has come to hold such an infamous place in Christian history, could thus be said to have begun in the interest of correct teaching.

With the Reformation came the attempt to return to a more "biblical" model for the church and thus a great revival of interest in biblical scholarship and teaching. The availability of the Scriptures in the common language raised all sorts of new problems. Just because laypersons could read the Bible did not mean they would understand it in the way their leaders wished. Indeed behind and through the entire Protestant impulse ran an emphasis on the individual's interpretation of scripture. Schools themselves became widespread in Protestant cultures at least partly in the attempt to teach the people to read so that they could read the Bible for themselves. And the universities of the New World were founded in a number of cases specifically to provide the people with an educated clergy. With the rise of different Protestant denominations came a proliferation of schools, each designed to provide the "correct" doctrinal training for their own clergy and lay leadership.

For the most part, of course, Christian teaching well into the nineteenth century continued to be done primarily in the churches by the clergy. Outside a specific preaching context, such teaching was largely catechetical. New converts, at whatever age, would be taught the basics of their chosen version of the faith. Beginning in Britain in 1781, however, the Sunday school movement would revolutionize the teaching process in the churches. The founding of the American Sunday School Union in 1824 began the process of providing regular literature.[12] That essentially Congregational organization was later duplicated by the Methodists, Baptists, and others.

The genius of the Sunday schools was the providing on a weekly basis in small groups of regular graded Bible instruction. Ahlstrom commented,

> In small towns and large cities they attracted dedicated lay leaders of great ability, helping to set the tone and temper of American Protestantism and providing an effective means of reaching the unchurched and unaffiliated–adults as well as children. Although they necessarily mirrored the country's values, the Sunday schools did produce a pious and knowledgeable laity on a scale unequaled anywhere in Christendom.[13]

In many ways it was the Sunday school movement that took Christian teaching for the broad range of Protestants out of the worship service and into a specific long-term structured context of its own. Even today for many American Christians the small group, whether it meets on Sunday morning or not and whether it studies the Bible or not, provides the basic unit of Christian instruction and fellowship.

Of course there are many other venues in which Christian teaching also takes place. Worship is one. Many preachers do a great deal of teaching in the context of the weekly round of services. In Baptist life, both Sunday evening and Wednesday evening services most often have the character of teaching rather than preaching experiences.

A great deal of Christian teaching is also done through the media. In fact, it is impossible to overestimate the impact of the media on Christian thought and perceptions in the last decade of the twentieth century. Radio and TV worship services and talk shows effectively communicate their creators' perspectives on the faith. Christian workbooks and video courses abound. There is an entire industry of Christian retreat centers and conferences promoting particular themes such as "family values." Christian magazines and newspapers disseminate the perspectives of various groups.

Teaching, as much as preaching, has come full circle in the sense that it is now, as it was in the beginning, a battleground for the hearts and minds of believers. In my own denomination of origin, the seminaries are in the process of radical restructuring by a takeover group that believes the traditional power structure has tolerated teaching that is doctrinally too liberal. The rules of denominational polity allow this.

The only objective controls that exist for the teaching process in a free society are the external limits of what the public and a particular confessional context will tolerate and the internal limits that Christian teachers impose upon themselves. It is therefore essential to be able to develop an ethics of teaching that may be applied whatever the context.

What direction does scripture offer in attempting to elaborate an ethics of teaching for today?

In the literary sense, the Bible is first and foremost a vehicle for teaching the spiritual life of a people. Through story and song and proverb and argument, scripture portrays the history of Judeo-Christian monotheism in a way designed to be followed by believers and shared with new converts. It is thus itself our primary example of ethical teaching. As such it allows a rather wide latitude for choosing means of teaching appropriate to particular contexts.

The Gospels themselves are a prime example of this. The primitive, essentially Hebrew narrative of Mark is put into a broader, more comprehensive context by Matthew, edited for a Gentile audience by Luke, and made more philosophically Greek for a later missionary generation by the writer of John. The Revelation to John takes the dramatic literary step of couching in apocalyptic language its message of encouragement for a generation under persecution. Thus an important part of the enduring message of the Bible itself has been the necessity of repackaging that essential message for the ears of each new group of hearers. Teaching must be contextual.

Teaching began as soon as the Hebrew people began. There must have been a time, a long time, when it was just the telling of the stories around the campfire–passing down the family history from generation to generation. With the giving of the Law, that history became more formalized. The cult needed not only to be observed but also to be understood. Hence the command of Deuteronomy 6:6-9.

> Keep these words that I am commanding you today in your heart. Recite them to your children and talk about them when you are at home and when you are away, when you lie down and when you rise. Bind them as a sign on your hand, fix them as an emblem on your forehead, and write them on the doorposts of your house and on your gates.

Here were specific teaching instructions indeed! The entire purpose of Hebrew life became to so surround the people with the knowledge of the Law that its observance became second nature. Even today observant Jews spend a lifetime studying the Law together with the rabbinical commentaries on it.

That the teaching of the law failed to produce righteousness is of course one theological underpinning for the New Testament. But the two look at teaching differently. In the Old Testament the burden of teaching is to pass on the accumulated wisdom of the people in its purest and most orthodox possible form. Even the prophets largely call the people back to earlier, stricter observance.

There is progress. Jeremiah 31 talks of individual rather than corporate responsibility for sin. There is the promise of a new covenant of the heart yet to come. Still the new message itself waits for a new day.

The chief ethical failing in Old Testament teaching is that of the lying prophets:

> And the Lord said to me: "The prophets are prophesying lies in my name; I did not send them, nor did I command them or speak to them." (Jer 14:14)

SURVIVING MINISTRY

To represent God falsely, without true experiential knowledge of the divine defines the essential sin of the unfaithful teacher. Old Testament scripture consistently condemns such conduct.

Much of Jesus' teaching follows a not-too-dissimilar line. In arguing against the practice of "corban," Jesus quoted the prophet Isaiah,

> This people honors me with their lips, but their hearts are far from me;
> in vain do they worship me, teaching human precepts as doctrines.
> (Matt 15:8-9)

He argued essentially that much of what is taught for piety actually has no root in God's Spirit.

Virtually all of Matthew 23 forms a diatribe against the scribes and Pharisees and the effect of their teaching. Jesus began by acknowledging their authority. "Do whatever they teach you and follow it; but do not do as they do, for they do not practice what they teach" (v. 3). But the gap between teaching and practice did not comprise the whole problem. They, who should have been teaching to liberate, "tie up heavy burdens, hard to bear, and lay them on the shoulders of others" (v. 4). They desired the respect given a teacher rather than actually helping people learn how to live. So angry was Jesus at this that he did away with the common titles of respect for those who teach. Today he would have said, "Call no one Doctor!"

The substance of what the scribes and Pharisees taught was actually so destructive as to keep others out of the kingdom of God (v. 13). That was Jesus' primary complaint. By their emphasis on the technical aspects of the Law, they missed

> the weightier matters of the law: justice and mercy and faith. It is these you ought to have practiced without neglecting the others. You blind guides! You strain out a gnat but swallow a camel! (vv. 23-24)

Teaching must communicate the essentials, or it is not true teaching.

The apostle James reminds us of the burden placed on teachers of the truth:

> Not many of you should become teachers, my brothers and sisters, for you know that we who teach will be judged with greater strictness. (Jas 3:1)

Thus we find that the church, with Jesus, fights a constant battle against false teaching. The writer of Timothy urged the young preacher to teach the teachers of the church to avoid getting sidetracked by the popular ideas of the day. They were "not to occupy themselves with myths and endless genealogies that promote speculations rather than divine training that is known by faith" (1 Tim 1:4). Jesus himself had observed,

> If any of you put a stumbling block before one of these little ones who believe in me, it would be better for you if a great millstone were hung around your neck and you were thrown into the sea. (Mark 9:42)

The sense of judgment thus held over teachers looms so great that one wonders why anyone would accept the job.

Yet teaching is also held to be one of the greatest privileges for a believer. In 1 Corinthians 12:26f, Paul places teaching third in his list of the spiritual gifts, ahead of deeds of power or healing or gifts of leadership in the church. One who wishes to be a bishop must be "an apt teacher" (1 Tim 3:2). Because teaching is such a privilege it must be exercised very carefully.

What are the ethics of teaching in the church?

It would be possible to summarize and say simply that Christian teaching to be ethical must be true. But we must unpack the nature of that truth in order to comprehend anything of how to teach ethically.

Part of the difficulty in the vignette with which we began is that Rev. Mack takes his own position as absolute truth and refuses to allow for disagreement. Clearly there exists a body of truth that is the obligation of Christian teachers to hold and communicate. The precise perceptions of the parameters of that body of truth vary widely from individual to individual and Christian community to Christian community. The definition of those parameters is the task of theology rather than ethics. Yet within each community they exist and exist to be taught. Jesus never hesitated to confront. Yet neither did he ever attempt to manipulate or to coerce agreement. Rev. Mack's teaching error was not that he held wrong convictions (although he did). His teaching error lay in failing to allow his student to disagree and to work toward a solution of his own. Ethical Christian teaching must by definition eschew coercion or manipulation.

Secondly, in Christian teaching the nature and conduct or character of the teacher is as important as the content of her teaching. When Jesus observes that the "disciple is not greater than his teacher," he reminds us that students are inherently hindered by, if not absolutely limited to, the degree of development of their teacher. This phenomenon is observable repeatedly in the churches.

People put their trust in a teacher or minister only to discover that person to be guilty of moral failure or of some other betrayal of the very truth he is claiming to teach. In the moment, the doctrines of the universality of sin and the necessity of grace are of little comfort. The results are disillusionment, cynicism, an interruption in or perhaps an actual abandonment of the Christian journey by the student. Recent years have seen this phenomenon seeming to become more common than ever. Except for one, every church I have served has witnessed this kind of betrayal by ministers or church leaders. The destructive effects cannot be overstated. Christ's harsh-sounding judgment for those who cause little ones to stumble seems decidedly less extreme when one has personally observed the results of the stumble.

In many ways the basic ethic of ministry, whatever else one does, must be like that of medicine, to do no harm. Hypocritical teaching, sloppy teaching, ill-prepared teaching, prejudicial teaching, manipulative teaching, exploitive teaching are all forbidden by this principle, which goes back ultimately to the New Testament's organizing principle of *agape* love.

A positive statement of the same ethic of no harm, crafted for the teaching environment, is to seek truth. In many ways the fault of the scribes and Pharisees was that they held to an old truth past its time. The true dynamic of teaching as a gift of the Spirit is rather, as Jesus said, to allow the Spirit to lead us "into all truth." The teacher must then be on the journey along with his or her students as all are led toward truth together.

At the level of theological debate, many Christian groups in the current arena face renewed tension over the nature of truth and how to find it. Fundamentalists and many evangelicals are in revolt against scholarly inquiry and theological innovation, which they see as an attack on biblical authority. Witness the uproar among fundamentalist Baptists over the issue of women in church leadership. Mainline churches are by no means exempt from the upheaval. The Presbyterian church, in particular, has been torn by reaction to an ecumenical "reimagining" conference held in 1994, which was designed to find new images for conceptualizing and speaking of God.

My contention would be that Jesus never did and never intended to limit us to first-century understandings of his truth. Indeed the purpose of the Spirit is in part to make certain we are not so limited. There are limits to innovation. But those limits are properly defined by the Spirit and nature of Christ and the purpose of redemption rather than by even the most sophisticated biblical prooftexting.

The third element in the ethics of Christian teaching is therefore the obligation to teach according to the truth, as one understands it. The problem with the teachers of Ephesus with whom Timothy dealt was that they had left that truth in order to occupy themselves with "myths and endless genealogies that promote speculations." Twentieth-century Christianity wanders through myriad examples of such diversions. The exclusive occupation with eschatology, glossalalia, the cultic diversions of Latter Day Saints and Jehovah's Witnesses, the late-century revival of rigid Calvinism, even the recent near-deification of the family, all represent to some degree the problem of majoring on minors.

This is not to be understood as in any way devaluing practical, social, or applied Christianity. Indeed a fervent concentration on the biblical salvation story, without application of the truths of that story to the lives of the hearers, may be just as perverted in its own way as any sect's special emphasis. In fact, people have often misused an appeal to Christian basics precisely to avoid taking seriously the implications and applications of those basics.

Our final point revisits our earlier observation concerning the contextual character of the biblical story. To be ethical, teaching must be appropriate and effective in its context. A well-meaning teacher who bores third-graders to death with college-level exegesis is not only inept but also unethical because such teaching does actual harm. It inoculates the students against receptiveness to further learning. Christian publishers, for example, who spew forth slick, brightly-colored materials that are not age-appropriate confuse the learning process. One publisher I know of habitually includes "salvation" lessons in material for four-year-olds, ignoring the fact that four-year-olds are not developmentally ready to absorb and respond appropriately to such concepts. That practice constitutes a "stumbling block" for one of Christ's dear ones if I ever saw it.

How should I approach
the ethics of counseling parishioners?

As he hurried his Lexus in the direction of the University Hospital's emergency room parking lot, Rev. Mack found his mind drawn inexorably toward the previous week's session with Linda.

She had seemed terribly depressed. Indeed at one point she had even begun talking about suicide, mentioned that she had a quantity of sleeping pills in her room. Mack had not taken many counseling classes at seminary, but he knew enough to recognize a serious situation when he saw it. He had tried to get Linda to talk about her feelings, and, when she grew silent, he had told her she must find a way to deal with whatever was bothering her.

"Linda, you can't go on like this. God doesn't want you to go on like this! You're just making yourself miserable. And suicide is a sin! That's no answer! I want you to go home, read the book of Philippians, and pray for guidance."

She just just sat there and looked at him. A beautiful young woman with the saddest face he had ever seen. As he ended the session with prayer, he found himself wondering if she were pregnant. But he dismissed the thought. Surely not after all his sermons about the dangers of premarital sex!

And now her parents had called him to the hospital. They had been summoned the night before when her dormmates found her unconscious. The doctors said she had taken a massive dose of sedatives and prospects for recovery were uncertain at best. She had lost her baby. If only she had listened! He parked his car and strode into the building.

How has the church dealt with the ethics of ministerial counseling?

Pastoral care, counseling, encouragement, spiritual direction—a great many similar activities in the church have traditionally come under the general heading of the work of the pastor. Only in the past half-century, though, has "pastoral care" become a kind of synonym for Christian psychology. Ministers have always counseled the confused, the seekers, and the grieving, but only with the rise of modern secular psychology has the church attempted to formalize training for pastoral care, establish standards for the profession, and apply a degree of clinical analysis to its practice both inside and outside the parish.

Still one cannot approach the subject without admitting that for much of church history there has been a mystique surrounding the personal work of the pastor in care of the congregation. Even in the churches of the radical Reformation—the Quakers and Baptists who have been most insistent on the priesthood of the believer and the concomitant equality of all believers—the clergy have played a significant role in representing the presence of God in the midst of the everyday life of the congregation.

In Catholicism, two practices symbolize the character and importance of the function of pastoral care. The first is the traditional "seal of the confessional." Pre-Vatican II Catholics were required to attend confession regularly in order to prepare themselves for communion. They were required to confess all known sin, receive priestly absolution, and perform whatever penance was prescribed. Any sin confessed and absolved within the confessional must remain confidential, blotted out by the blood of Christ. It is easy to see how that practice must lead to an unburdening of souls, and, with perceptive and compassionate priests, a kind of rough-and-ready counseling ministry.

The second practice, arising out of the monastic life, is that of "spiritual direction." In spiritual direction, a novice in the faith comes under the watchcare of an older, more spiritually experienced believer. That director acts as both confessor and guide. More popular with clergy than laity, the practice of spiritual direction nonetheless provides an archetype of the kind of pastoral counseling that is more commonly undertaken today.

In Reformation Protestantism, a vital section of ministerial work was devoted to the "care of souls."[14] Pauck describes a regular regimen of visitation of the sick and of those in need of counsel for the perfection of their Christian lives. This practice was built into the structure of the Genevan ministry and emulated in many corners of Europe and later America. George Herbert's country parson maintained a similar round in seventeenth-century England.

> The Country Parson, when any of his cure is sick, or afflicted with loss of friend, or estate, or any ways distressed, fails not to afford his best comforts, and rather goes to them, than sends for the afflicted, though they can, and otherwise ought to come to him. To this end he hath thoroughly digested all the points of consolation, as having continual use of them, such as are from God's general providence extended even to lilies; from his particular, to his Church; from his promise, from the examples of all Saints that ever were; from Christ himself, perfecting our Redemption no other way, than by sorrow; from the Benefit of affliction, which softens, and works the stubborn heart of man; from the certainty both of deliverance, and reward, if we faint not; from the miserable comparison of the moment of griefs here with the weight of joys hereafter. Besides this, in his visiting the sick, or otherwise afflicted, he followeth the Church's counsel, namely in persuading them in particular confession, laboring to make them

understand the great good use of this ancient and pious ordinance, and how necessary it is in some cases; he also urgeth them to do some pious charitable works, as a necessary evidence and fruit of their faith, at that time especially.[15]

The success of such work appears always to have depended upon the perception and sensitivity of the individual practitioner, though the ministers did have a powerful weapon in their arsenals. Since it was they who either admitted or refused a person access to communion, except for the free churches, they were believed quite literally to hold the "keys of the kingdom." Those who refused to accept their counsel could be kept from the comforts of the church.

In nineteenth-century Baptist churches, especially those of the revivalist or "Sandy Creek" tradition, this process of repentance and restoration took place often in front of the whole body of the church. Church minutes of the era are full of references to brother or sister so-and-so having danced or drunk and been forgiven or sometimes not. That such practices did violence to personal privacy needs hardly be noted for a twentieth-century audience. But they arose in a time when the community was a much more important concept in American culture than it is today.

Today, with the exception of occasional revivals, which meet with mixed reception, the process of counseling believers most often takes place either in their home or the minister's office. An entire industry of professional pastoral counselors, who operate either in conjunction with particular congregational ministerial staffs or independently, has grown up to serve a Christian population still somewhat suspicious of secular psychology.

Beginning in about 1950, with the writing and teaching of pioneers such as Wayne Oates and Seward Hiltner, pastoral care has become an increasingly professional discipline. It stands with one foot in Christian teaching and the other in psychological research and theory. Frequently those who enter seminary thinking they will become parish ministers find themselves instead entering into pastoral care practice in Christian hospitals or counseling groups. Along with this movement has come an increasing suspicion of the traditional, rather rough-and-ready blend of spiritual counsel and common sense with which most ministers have greeted their parishioners' problems. It is certainly true that most seminary curriculae include in their requirements for basic ministerial degrees only one or two courses in pastoral care and little or no direct supervision in its practice. The primary critique of Rev. Mack that many would make is that he was counseling beyond his training and should have referred the young woman to a "professional."

All of this, for ministers who do not intend to specialize in pastoral care but recognize an obligation for professionalism and integrity in the care of souls, raises serious ethical issues. What subjects may a minister not extensively trained in pastoral care legitimately address? When should one refer a counselee, and to whom? Should you always recommend a specifically Christian psychologist? What about when scriptural teaching and the best modern psychological theory conflict?

What help does scripture offer in developing an ethics of counseling for ministers today?

In some ways both the best and the worst examples of biblical counseling technique are embodied in the story of Job.

> Now when Job's three friends heard of all these troubles that had come upon him, each of them set out from his home—Eliphaz the Temanite, Bildad the Shuhite, and Zophar the Naamathite. They met together to go and console and comfort him. When they saw him from a distance, they did not recognize him, and they raised their voices and wept aloud; they tore their robes and threw dust in the air upon their heads. They sat with him on the ground seven days and seven nights, and no one spoke a word to him, for they saw that his suffering was very great. (Job 2:11-13)

There is no better statement of the counseling ministry of presence. Sometimes the most and the best a counselor can do is be present with someone in their pain. On the other hand, these same three friends were certain that Job's problems must in some fashion be the result of some sin of his rather than of a set of circumstances beyond his control. Their priggish self-righteousness became his burden rather than his help. There will indeed be times when ministers are called to help someone recognize their own sin. But the statement of judgment must be carefully done and only in the face of certainty on the part of the Christian counselor. Otherwise, it becomes damaging rather than helpful.

Christian ministers in some evangelical circles particularly seem to be attempting to follow the example of Jesus in pronouncing regarding the spiritual health and needs of their parishoners. I have known ministers to forbid certain members to marry each other, to counsel people to change jobs, or to suggest members cut ties with their families of origin for the sake of their spiritual "well-being."

Certainly it is true that Jesus, on small acquaintance, proffered rather radical prescriptions for a number of people he encountered. The "rich young ruler" story comes particularly to mind. Jesus advised the young man to sell all his many possessions and give the proceeds to the poor in order to attain spiritual peace (Matt 19:16-22). One would hardly expect any counselor in any conceivable modern setting to offer such a radical prescription. But the counselor must always remember he was Jesus, and we are not. Christian counseling seeks clarity of understanding, but it cannot impose authoritative solutions. The biblical stories assume a supernatural depth and insight in Jesus that we do not possess as a birthright and that we may approach only in our most sensitively spiritual moments.

All of this raises the question of whether there may be said to exist an appropriately biblical goal for Christian counseling as distinct from secular psychiatric or psychological praxis. Certainly there is much the disciplines share. All seek the health of the counselee. But Christian counseling, as practiced in the parish setting, remains distinct in purpose. Christian counseling seeks the spiritual welfare of the counselee, a goal that includes but goes beyond many of the issues normally addressed in secular counseling.

When Jesus addressed the myriad personal and social problems of his day, he did so always in terms of the relationship to God of those with whom he dealt.

> The Pharisees and their scribes were complaining to his disciples, saying, "Why do you eat and drink with tax collectors and sinners?" Jesus answered, "Those who are well have no need of a physician, but those who are sick; I have come to call not the righteous but sinners to repentance." (Luke 5:30-31)

That is perhaps the central thing a Christian minister must remember. People seek a pastoral counselor in the first place because they wish to work out their problems in the context of their relationship with God. To fail to focus on this is to deny the whole purpose and function of pastoral care.

Jesus undertook his pastoral counseling in two specific ways. The first we have already alluded to above. That is the call to repentance and appropriate penitential action. The rich young man in Matthew 19 was called to sell his possessions and give to the poor, we surmise, because he had been living a lifestyle of lavish self-indulgence. The act of selling his possessions was required to divorce him from old priorities. The act of giving to the poor was a penitential reconnection with those he may have exploited or discounted in the past.

The second specific technique Jesus used was the dispensation of grace. In the story of the healing of the paralytic (Luke 5), the sick man was brought to Jesus by friends who went to the extreme of tearing a hole in the roof of the crowded building where Jesus was and lowering the sick man through the hole. "When he saw their faith, he said, 'Friend, your sins are forgiven you' " (v. 20). Again and again, much to the dismay of the legalistic scribes and Pharisees, Jesus offered forgiveness for sin in the process of healing physical illnesses. He clearly saw a real connection between healing and the reception of grace. Theologians and physicians have been attempting to understand the precise nature of that connection ever since. For Jesus it was direct and spiritual.

In some ways Paul appears to have perverted Jesus' simple understanding by setting the church up for the development of the very gnosticism he railed against. For Paul, existence "in Christ" was so different as to be a separate state altogether from nonChristian life.

> Those who are unspiritual do not receive the gifts of God's Spirit, for they are foolishness to them, and they are unable to understand them because they are spiritually discerned. Those who are spiritual discern all things, and they are themselves subject to no one else's scrutiny. (1 Cor 2:14-15)

The danger is that Christians are set such high expectations both by themselves and by others that they will not allow themselves to admit to human failings. My own branch of Protestant pietism long preached that Jesus would solve all your problems and ignored or denied the struggles of church members when they arose. Still today seeing a counselor is in many settings viewed as a suspicious act.

Paul admitted, however, that things are not always so simple. Coming to Christ does not cause one's problems to disappear.

> For we know that the law is spiritual; but I am of the flesh, sold into slavery under sin. I do not understand my own actions. For I do not do what I want, but I do the very thing I hate. . . . For I know that nothing good dwells within me, that is, in my flesh. I can will what is right, but I cannot do it. (Rom 7:14-15, 18-19)

In this sense Christian counseling seeks to aid the believer in the life-long struggle to inculcate grace and repentance into the fabric of one's life.

When Christ gave the twin commandments to love God and to love the neighbor as oneself, he set the parameters for the goal of Christian counseling. Following Barnette, we have defined *agape* love as "willing and working for the well-being" of the person loved. That comprehensive well-being is the objective of Christian counseling. It is akin to the Old Testament concept of *shalom. Shalom* represents a wholistic concept of well-being that includes peace but also prosperity and satisfaction. Christian counseling hopes to assist the believer in achieving that kind of general well-being.

How do we construct an ethics of counseling for ministers today?

The above treatment of biblical principles leads us to several specific observations regarding ministers in their role as counselor. First, absent specific clinical training, ministers should restrict their counseling practice to matters of spiritual well-being. In that sense, the minister's first ethical obligation in counseling is to have enough counseling training to be able to recognize when a counselee should be referred to a professional provider. Rev. Mack in our opening vignette failed to recognize the severity of his counselee's problem and thereby contributed to the crisis that followed.

It should be noted as well that this is not only an ethical matter for ministerial counselors. It is ethical because ministers are committed to providing the best possible care for their parishoners. To fail to provide access to that care is to fail in the ministerial task. But it is also professional. There is an increasing body of case law in which ministers have been sued for malpractice with regard to failed counseling situations.

Thus the ministers' initial commitment to do no harm serves as a boundary between those situations in which they will do the counseling themselves and those in which they will refer to more qualified practitioners. For parish ministers with basic seminary training, this point cannot be overemphasized. It is unloving, irresponsible, and unethical to proceed when you lack sufficient skills to do so.

Second is a related point. Because of the minister's powerful situation with regard to counselees from within the congregation, there is a special obligation not to abuse the counseling situation for personal purposes.[16] It is almost commonplace to hear of situations in which a minister has become sexually involved with a counselee. Such involvement violates the most basic obligation to seek the well-being of the counselee. Ministers who fall into this abuse need extensive treatment accompanied by an extended hiatus in their ministerial responsibilities.

Third, within the context of those appropriate counseling situations, ministers should keep in mind the primary goal of the spiritual welfare of the counselee. The entrepreneurial character of contemporary ministry tempts many ministers to use counseling situations to build personal or institutional loyalty in the counselee. Yet there may well be times when ministers must speak the truth, even though a relationship is jeapordized thereby, and there will also be times when they may need to advise a counselee to leave a parish setting for his or her own well-being. Ministers need to remain extremely clear-minded concerning the pressures and motivations they themselves bring to a counseling situation.

Fourth, therefore, a minister should not ask any congregant to submit to a counseling process to which the minister does not also submit. Ministers who do counseling need also to be in counseling on a regular basis themselves. That counsel may be as informal as a ministerial support group or as formal as a clinical relationship with a professional. But it should also include ongoing training in counseling technique. I have often thought the apostle Paul, had he been willing to learn, would have benefited greatly from clinical pastoral education.

Fifth, the time given to a minister's counseling practice should be weighed against the time needed to accomplish the many other tasks in congregational life. A pastor who spends all her time counseling cannot also administer, study, prepare sermons, and attend to other forms of pastoral care. Generally speaking, ministers who want to develop an extensive counseling ministry should get out of parish responsibilities in order to do that. Otherwise, both areas will suffer. This point supports those congregations that have established specific positions for counselors within or adjunct to the church staff. This function has become so specialized that it is often best left to those specifically focused upon it.

Sixth, with the goal of spiritual well-being in mind, the minister's obligation is to speak "the truth in love." Paul made this doctrinal point:

> We must no longer be children, tossed to and fro and blown about by every wind of doctrine, by people's trickery, by their craftiness in deceitful scheming. But speaking the truth in love, we must grow up in

every way into him who is the head, into Christ, from whom the whole body, joined and knit together by every ligament with which it is equipped, as each part is working properly, promotes the body's growth in building itself up in love. (Eph 4:14-16)

The application has a broader validity, however. Whether a parishioner's problem is doctrinal confusion, or a particular sin, or a relational failing, the minister's obligation, as kindly as possible, is to help that person see and understand the problem in order that he or she may grow in Christ.

This is quite different from such secular approaches as "nondirective" or nonvalue-driven counseling. The minister approaches the counseling session, as does the counselee who seeks a minister, from the specific perspective of Christian growth. The road to that growth may be long and tortuous, but its presence as a goal should never be forgotten. The healing and wholeness goals of secular counseling may be in tune with Christian goals in specific situations, but they do not share ultimate values.

From this perspective, Rev. Mack's goal of Linda's spiritual welfare was acceptable. His fault lay in failing to perceive the depth of her depression, in failing to provide her the kind of grace-filled atmosphere in which she would have felt safe confiding in him about her pregnancy, and in failing to refer her to a more clinically trained counselor. There may be counselees for whom instruction to read the book of Philippians is sufficient. Linda was not one of those, and Rev. Mack should have recognized it.

Had she confided in him, however, and had she not been so seriously depressed, he might have chosen to engage her in dialogue about her core values. How did she feel about what she had done? Did she have an obligation to the baby? To the baby's father? What would be the responsible Christian thing to do given her situation? Christian counseling need not be afraid to bring to bear Christian values. That is at least a portion of its purpose.

In our own poor way, Christian counselors seek to be Christ's ears and voice for the people of our churches. As such we cannot escape the tension between the call to responsibility and the offering of grace. Each is a valid part of Christian pastoral care. Each is appropriate in some situations and not in others. Neither must be allowed to dominate the counseling process to the exclusion of the other. In the final chapter of our framework for ethics in ministry, we will examine the tension between grace and demand in a slightly different way. How does the minister deal with the sometimes disturbing ethical demands of the faith in the context of a parish and its personal and institutional needs? We look at the problem of prophecy.

Notes

[1]Raymond H. Bailey, "Ethics in Preaching," *Review and Expositor* (Fall 1989) 86:534

[2]George H. Williams, "The Ministry in the Later Patristic Period," in *The Ministry in Historical Perspective*, H. Richard Niebuhr, ed. (New York: Harper & Row, 1983) 71.

[3]Ibid., 72.

[4]Ibid., 73.

[5]Bailey, 533-34.

[6]Ibid., 535-36. Bailey actually includes a list of five issues in the section of his article in which he deals with plagiarism, but he clearly considers plagiarism to be a separate and essentially parallel issue.

[7]Gaylord Noyce, *Pastoral Ethics* (Nashville: Abingdon, 1988) 51-52.

[8]Ibid., 67.

[9]John Knox, "The Ministry in the Primitive Church," in *The Ministry in Historical Perspective*, 14.

[10]"The Didache," quoted in *Documents of the Christian Church*, 2nd. ed., Henry Bettenson, ed. (Oxford: Oxford University Press, 1967) 65.

[11]Justin, "Apology," quoted in *Documents of the Christian Church*, 67.

[12]Sydney E. Ahlstrom, *A Religious History of the American People*, vol. 1 (Garden City NY: Image Books, 1975) 516.

[13]Ibid., vol. 2, 199.

[14]Wilhelm Pauck, "Ministry in the Time of the Continental Reformation," in *The Ministry in Historical Perspective*, 136.

[15]George Herbert, "The Country Parson," in George Herbert, *The Country Parson, The Temple,* John N. Wall, Jr., ed. (New York: Paulist Press, 1981) 77.

[16]The book *Sex in the Forbidden Zone* by Peter Rutter, M.D. (New York: Ballantine Books, 1989) explores the abuse of power in counseling situations by ministers and other professionals.

CHAPTER 6
PROPHECY

Christian ethicists, whether they will admit it or not, commonly think of themselves as the true heirs of the prophetic tradition. It is appropriate, therefore, to round out our framework for ethics in ministry with an examination of ways in which the prophetic tradition is and is not respected in the practice of ministry today. Since prophecy is properly defined not as foretelling but rather as "forth-telling" the truth and its consequences for our lives, we will be dealing at the intersection between the minister's practical institutional obligations to his or her congregation and the obligation to speak forth the gospel as he or she understands it. Without apology, this chapter is in some ways perhaps the most personal of the book. Ultimately, all I can tell you is what I am learning in the process of ministerial practice.

What ethics apply to my practice of evangelism in seeking to help a church grow?

"Let's review this month's statistics!" The staff all groaned inwardly as the church board began what had become an all-too-familiar and depressing ritual.

The simple truth was Highview Hill was in decline. A century-old, theologically progressive congregation in a stable neighborhood, Highview Hill had not wanted to adopt the contemporary worship, casual dress, and cultural conservatism of its more suburban neighbor parishes. But a 15 percent drop in membership over the past five years had created almost unbearable pressure for change. Board meetings had become fraught with tension. Tonight, there was confrontation in the air.

"This is insupportable!" Ben Johnson broke out as soon as Mary Hildreth finished the report. "We're down in every category again! If we don't turn this church around soon, there's not going to be anyone left to hear these reports!"

"We've got to recruit more members!" Ben's son Bill chimed in. "When is the staff going to adopt new evangelism techniques like they're using at Southwest? I hear they're up 10 percent this year!"

"Now Bill," senior pastor Louis McEnrow cautioned, "we've been through all this before. We've agreed we don't want to give up the hymnal. You've all said you want me to keep preaching as I do. Southwest is strictly consumer-oriented. People join there because nobody asks them to change."

"Well, at least they join, Pastor," Bill shot back, too upset to be polite. "We've had more deaths the past two years than we've had additions! At this rate we'll be holding worship in the cemetery."

Next morning the five members of the ministerial staff all seemed to need to debrief, so McEnrow called a coffee-break conference in the church parlor. After everyone had groused about the Johnson family for what seemed the hundredth time, though, McEnrow shocked them all.

"I know how you all feel," he said, "and I agree we don't want to compromise on this. But what we're doing obviously isn't working. I want each of you to come back to me in two weeks with five ideas for making our church more appealing to newcomers. We've got to reach more people. And if we have to borrow from Southwest, so be it! Our job is to grow this church. Now let's get to work!"

How can we characterize the history of the issues of evangelism and church growth?

In one sense, of course, evangelism is what the history of the Christian church has been about. From the moment of Christ's Great Commission to the disciples (Matt 28:19-20), *the* agenda of the church has been to grow, to extend the gospel to all people everywhere. From the moment of the coming of the Holy Spirit at Pentecost, that task has been characterized by what Frank Stagg calls the "unhindering" of the gospel.[1] Women, all races, the disabled were all welcomed into the fellowship before the conclusion of the book of Acts.

Once the church became the church of the Roman Empire after Constantine, that evangelism was often accomplished by the wholesale baptism of entire peoples into the faith, whether they understood what was happening or not. Typical missionary strategy was to attempt to convert the ruler of a nation, who would then forcibly or by edict convert its people. The church then took on the monumental task of educating its converts in what the faith was all about. As late as the colonization of Latin America, the Roman church was still using a kind of conversion by conquest as one of its principal evangelistic techniques.

With the identification of church and government in Christendom and the virtually universal acceptance of the Judeo-Christian worldview in the West, the church came to expect the faithful to seek out confession, absolution, and communion rather than to feel a compulsion to engage in extensive evangelism. The monastics provided a way for those who sought a higher Christian life. Ordinary laity were expected simply to be faithful and obedient.

There were always, of course, pockets of believers whose views were unorthodox and who sought to win converts to their way of thinking. They enjoyed varying degrees of toleration depending upon the degree of threat felt by the established church.

The two changes in Western civilization that created the modern issues of church growth and evangelism were the Protestant Reformation and the Enlightenment, its intellectual companion. The Reformation, with its heavy emphasis on the individual, led to an increasing religious pluralism in the English-speaking world. The British concept of religious toleration and the American idea of the separation of church and state led to a kind of free market economy of religion in which each church's ideas must compete for converts. At the same time, the Enlightenment dethroned theology from its traditional place as the "queen of the sciences" and introduced secularism as a growing force. It became intellectually respectable to espouse no religion at all.

In the New World, particularly, out of the reach of England's parishes, frontier life worked against church involvement. The Great Awakening, the first of the American evangelistic outbursts took place partially because a large portion of the American population had become ignorant of the claims of the faith. The Methodists and Baptists grew in frontier America precisely because they adapted their methods to the needs of the frontier. The Methodists developed their system of small groups, revival meetings, and circuit-riding preachers. The Baptists used the even more egalitarian farmer-preachers. Taking the gospel message where the people were and presenting it in simple, culture-specific terms, these two churches came to dominate the American frontier.

Along with the more education-oriented Presbyterians and Congregationalists, these American churches created a system of schools and colleges for the training of ministers and the Christian education of laity. They founded hospitals, orphanages, and various kinds of reform societies to meet human needs. They created mission societies to take the gospel to foreign lands. Till the coming of the great Catholic immigration of the late nineteenth and early twentieth centuries, they dominated the American religious scene.

The Sunday school movement and the forces of denominationalism were powerful evangelistic tools in the early part of this century. Sunday schools brought into contact with the gospel many who were not otherwise churched. Groups such as Southern Baptists used membership campaigns to great advantage. "A Million More in Fifty Four" is one prime example of such a campaign.

As the twentieth century has worn on, however, the forces of secularism have become ever more powerful in American life. Revivalism, once a powerful mainstream American phenomenon, has become more and more culturally suspect. With the exposure and disgrace of many TV evangelists in recent years, public cynicism concerning religion has grown rampant. Denominationalism, once a powerful motivating force in American religion, is waning. With the disputes in many denominations between "conservatives" and "liberals," the public has grown increasingly suspicious of denominational labels. The phenomenon of media-fed "megachurches," usually independent of any denominational label, has led some congregations to drop denominational labels from their names. In some groups, traditional worship has gone out of fashion as an informal, quasi-secular style has replaced coats with shirt sleeves, organs with synthesizers, anthems with praise choruses, and biblical expositions with topical "needs-oriented" sermons. All of these changes have created unprecedented challenges for churches that seek both to survive institutionally and to share the gospel with a new generation.

Traditionalists charge that the new evangelistic efforts have perverted the gospel in the interest of making it consumer-oriented. Innovators charge that traditionalists do not care as much about real people as they do about church tradition. Responsible ministers such as Louis McEnrow have to somehow preserve what needs to be preserved and change what needs to be changed. For many, this has become an issue of the ethics of ministeral practice. Every congregation I have ever served has faced some version of this challenge. Every ministerial student who reads this book will have to find some way to deal with this issue.

What biblical insights inform an ethics of evangelism in the local church?

Evangelism is a peculiarly Christian and therefore peculiarly New Testament phenomenon. The Jews saw themselves as God's people by birthright. They were a light to the nations rather than a people bent on inclusion. They accepted converts when converts came, but they felt no particular obligation to seek them when they did not. God's promise that in Abraham "all the families of the earth will be blessed" (Gen 12:3) was seen as God's business to accomplish and not the Jews'.

Christ's imperative to share the good news is thus something new in the stream of Judeo-Christian history. That he made it the single, central, universal purpose of the church in the Great Commission cannot be overemphasized. It is also significant that the Holy Spirit, who in the pre-crucifixion scenes of the Gospel of John is portrayed as comforter and as guide into truth, was promised at the ascension primarily as a source of power for the purpose of evangelism (Acts 1:8). When the Holy Spirit actually came to the disciples (Acts 2), the immediate result was explosive growth in the church.

Paul confirmed this central evangelistic purpose of the church not only by his own life, but also by his writings, for example, 1 Corinthians 9:19-23.

> For though I am free with respect to all, I have made myself a slave to all, so that I might win more of them. To the Jews I became as a Jew, in order to win Jews. To those under the law I became as one under the law (though I myself am not under the law) so that I might win those under the law. To those outside the law I became as one outside the law (though I am not free from God's law but am under Christ's law) so that I might win those outside the law. To the weak I became weak, so that I might win the weak. I have become all things all people, that I might by all means save some. I do it all for the sake of the gospel, so that I may share in its blessings.

The methodology Paul espoused is thus pragmatic in the extreme. To state it bluntly, whatever works to win genuine converts is acceptable as an evangelistic tool. Indeed, it is the obligation of the Christian to seek out and find those techniques that work in a given situation, and use them.

It is also true that there is a distinct difference between the institution of the church as it is known today and the church of New Testament times. Christ himself only referred to the church a couple of times, in passages the authenticity of which has sometimes been disputed. The church of the Epistles was a fluid grouping of believers and seekers, meeting wherever it was possible or convenient, with very few of the institutional obligations or characteristics of the modern church. Only in the later Pastoral Epistles do significant structural aspects begin to emerge. Some argue from this fact that the modern church is "not biblical" and therefore not worth protecting in particular institutional expressions.

Evangelism, even in the New Testament, however, does have specific content. In his letters to the church at Corinth, for example, Paul struggles to define true gospel teaching as over against various corrupting ideas and influences that have grown up since his departure. The church by its very nature "institutionalizes" its ways of thinking and acting very quickly indeed. To fail to recognize that those ways of thinking and acting must somehow be managed and controlled is to fall victim to naivete. Loyalty to "whatever works" must in some measure be governed by a prior loyalty to "what is true."

In John, chapter 6, Christ himself experiences a falling away of many of his earlier disciples because of his teaching regarding eating his flesh and drinking his blood. It was a truth that those who heard were not willing to accept. In the book of Acts, Paul suffers repeatedly because both Jews and Gentiles reject the content of his message.

Pragmatism clearly does not extend, therefore, to altering the content of the gospel message itself, only its packaging for specific situations. This is the point upon which much of the debate between more institutional and more pragmatic approaches to evangelism hinges. Those who defend the institutional church argue that the pragmatic churches lose too much of the content of the message in their desire to spread it as broadly as possible. Those who defend the pragmatic approach tend to minimize cultivation of Christian maturity in the headlong rush to make as many converts as possible.

We do find some scriptural balance in the author of 2 Timothy's counsel to the young minister. On the one hand, Timothy was told to "do your best to present yourself to God as one approved by him, a worker who has no need to be ashamed, rightly explaining the word of truth." (2 Tim 2:15). On the other hand, he was to "proclaim the message; be persistent whether the time is favorable or unfavorable" (2 Tim 4:2). Tempered by truth, evangelism remains a primary task.

Evangelism, further, requires a depth and intensity of commitment not always true of modern institutional Christianity. In 2 Corinthians 11, Paul defends the sincerity of his own commitment to Christ.

> Are they ministers of Christ? . . . I am a better one: with far greater labors, far more imprisonments, with countless floggings, and often near death. Five times I have received from the Jews the forty lashes

minus one. Three times I was beaten with rods. Once I received a stoning. Three times I was shipwrecked; for a night and a day I was adrift at sea. . . . And, besides other things, I am under daily pressure because of my anxiety for all the churches. Who is weak and I am not weak? Who is made to stumble and I am not indignant? (vv. 23-25, 28-29)

Much of the evangelistic energy of institutional churches in America and England has often been drained off into the foreign missions enterprise. Their inherently risky character has seemed more reminiscent of Paul than the relatively tame demands of the domestic church.

We must consider one further difference between New Testament times and our own. Paul and, as far as we know, all the other first-century Christians joined Jesus in expecting an early end to this present world. That eschatological expectation lent an urgency to their evangelistic work that is occasionally found in more sectarian expressions of modern Christendom. It is not, however, characteristic of the mainstream. Most Christians of the late twentieth century have simply ceased expecting Jesus to come again soon in any meaningful sense beyond the entry of individuals into eternity at their death. *Pro forma* expression is given to the expectation, but it cannot be said to be a motivating factor in evangelism except in very specific situations.

How do we construct an
ethic of evangelism for the church today?

Pastor McEnrow's dilemma is repeated across the board in churches today. Some say as many as 85 percent of the congregations in America are in decline in the 1990s. Many of those not in decline are those that have adapted themselves as much as possible to secular culture in the pursuit of "church growth."

The first principle would seem to me to draw upon Paul's idea that evangelism by its very nature must be suited to the context. In older, established churches the faith has taken on an expression that verges on being a culture of its own. Hardly any unchurched American in the last years of the twentieth century can even define "invocation" or "doxology," much less participate comfortably while these things take place.

There are cultural reasons why Highview Hill grew in earlier years and why it is not growing now. It is incumbent upon Pastor McEnrow and his staff to try to understand what those reasons for earlier growth were and whether they still apply to the situation as it stands. If they do, it may be that a return to attention to earlier priorities could produce the increased effectiveness they seek.

If earlier conditions no longer apply, then it becomes the ministers' task to lead the church to understand the new culture under which they find themselves and to adapt their approach to evangelism in order to be effective under those new conditions. Having said that, it is important to remember, though, that no church can do everything. Neither could Paul, despite his assertions to the contrary.

What is more practical, and therefore more ethical, is for a particular congregation to decide what niche it occupies in the local "market," what constituents it can best reach, and to concentrate its efforts on reaching that group. This does not mean that a church should write off some individuals or groups as "not our job." It does mean that no church, no matter how large or diverse or talented, has the resources to meet every need or reach every nonbeliever in its community. Even Paul admitted that he only won "some."

A second principle is that evangelism must convey the truth of the faith in a balanced and comprehensive manner. No congregation has the right to skew its presentation of the gospel for the sake of bringing in new members.

Any number of commonly used contemporary tactics could be construed as unethical given this principle. The practice of one Chicago area church of taping money under certain seats on the church bus in order to attract children conveys ideas antithetical to the gospel. It is a rank abuse of innocence. Also antithetical to true gospel understanding is the even more common identification of the gospel with American patriotism. Christ's gospel stands above and beyond all nationalism for whatever nation. A third dangerous tactic is the idea conveyed by many megachurches that the Christian faith guarantees success in business or in family life. History and the gospel demonstrate otherwise, but the tactic sells, so it is still frequently used.

It should be noted that this principle does not necessarily criticize many evangelistic methods that some people, including this author, might find offensive. Knocking on doors is not excluded thereby. Neither is the "Evangelism Explosion" approach that asks the question "If you died tonight, where would you be tomorrow?" Such tricks of the trade fail the pragmatic test rather than an ethical one. They often fail to present a picture of the gospel that is winsome enough to be attractive to potential converts. Most people these days simply do not like someone knocking on their door without an appointment, and they tend to react negatively to whatever the uninvited guest proposes.

A third ethical principle for evaluating evangelism might be called the "Gamaliel" principle. Our tendency in current life is to decide immediately whether an approach is appropriate or not. Gamaliel suggested to the Sanhedrin, however, that by moving too hastily toward judgment they might be found to be opposing God.

Some things are clearly inappropriate. The activities of "TV evangelists" more interested in their viewers' money than their spiritual well-being should be condemned by serious Christians everywhere. But with regard to movements such as the attempt to present the gospel in terms of popular culture, more traditional Christians would do well to wait to see how deep and genuine is the faith such efforts produce long-term.

The same can be said of contemporary-minded Christians' evaluations of more traditional approaches. The issue at last is not exclusively how one worships or the terms by which one presents Christ to outsiders. The issue is whether or not one's method of evangelism represents an authentic enough picture of Christ to result in robust, balanced, and growing faith among the people one's work touches. If so, that evangelistic approach may be said to be generally acceptable. If not, time itself becomes the judge.

Such a principle does not, however, ignore the earlier statement that the picture of the gospel must be authentic. One of the most successful and enduring American religious phenomena is the Church of Jesus Christ of Latter Day Saints. The "Mormons" have built themselves a healthy and growing empire. But they are not orthodox Christians, and no amount of success can make them so. The ethics of evangelism must always be guarded by the authenticity of the message itself.

It is entirely appropriate ethically for Pastor McEnrow to ask his staff to come up with new approaches to their task. It is appropriate, should they decide there remains an adequate potential constituency, for Highview Hill to remain a traditionally oriented congregation. It is also appropriate for their sister congregations to have adopted more contemporary methodologies. It is not appropriate, however, to change, eviscerate, misrepresent, or abuse the truth of the gospel for the sake of a broader appeal.

How hard should I push
a church toward theologically correct but
unpopular social action ministry?

The phone had not stopped ringing all morning. Children's minister Sheila Armstrong hung up wearily from her eighth irate parent of the day and made her way to Pastor Jane Allen's office to report.

"I don't think we can do it," she moaned, slumping rather than sitting down on Allen's couch. "The Edwards have just threatened to leave if we go ahead. That's three children. She teaches Sunday School, and he's a substantial contributor. Can we afford to lose them for this family we don't even know?"

It had all started innocently enough. Six months before, as part of the AIDS support network in town, First Church had instituted "universal precautions" in the preschool Sunday School. The argument was they wanted to be ready if a child infected with AIDS wanted to attend Sunday School.

But now Annie had come along. A bright, vivacious three-year-old, Annie had contracted the HIV virus from her mother, who must have been infected by a blood transfusion ten years ago. She'd had no idea, no symptoms until Annie tested positive at birth. And now with a death sentence hanging over mother and daughter, the family was looking for a place to worship.

Suddenly Christian theory needed to become practice for First Church, and the preschool parents had erupted into panic.

"What do we do, Jane?" Sheila asked, in tears. "I can't turn Annie away. I'll resign first! What will you say to the church?"

Jane turned around in her chair and looked out the window toward the church playground. "I wish I knew," she answered. "I wish I knew!"

What is the history of the balance
between social action and aquiescence in the church?

H. Richard Niebuhr wrote the classic statement on *Christ and Culture,* identifying five historical types for the interaction between the church and the particular cultural milieu within which it finds itself. The dialogue, he argues, is perpetual.

> In his single-minded direction toward God, Christ leads men (sic) away from the temporality and pluralism of culture. In its concern for the conservation of the many values of the past, culture rejects the

Christ who bids men rely on grace. Yet the Son of God is himself child of a religious culture and sends his disciples to tend his lambs and sheep, who cannot be guarded without cultural work. The dialogue proceeds with denials and affirmations, reconstructions, compromises, and new denials. Neither individual nor church can come to a stopping-place in the endless search for an answer which will not provoke a new rejoinder.[2]

Niebuhr's types–Christ above culture, Christ of culture, Christ against culture, Christ and culture in paradox, and Christ transforming culture– suggest different ways in which the church has dealt with the challenges and critiques the gospel brings to bear. For purposes of understanding the dilemma we ministers face, we will provide a historical sketch of the church's experience with one particular social issue, that of war and peace.

In the early years, of course, the church was pacifist for a number of reasons. Jesus himself taught an ethic of radical nonviolence. But as Roland Bainton said,

The pacifism of the early church was derived not from a New Testament legalism, but from an effort to apply what was taken to be the mind of Christ.[3]

As an essentially spiritual movement, looking for an early end to this present world, the church eschewed politics. As time went on, of course, more and more military folk began to be converted. They were faced with the ethical dilemma of whether they could continue in their profession and follow Christ.

The conversion of Constantine thrust the church into the realm of power politics whether it wanted to be there or not. Pacifism was still an important thread in Christian teaching, but, as has always been the case, Christians began to search the Scriptures for texts more supportive of what they were actually doing. Two additional threads began to work their way into the fabric of Christian theology.

As the dominant religion of the later Empire, Christians clearly had an interest in maintaining the status quo. Bainton said that it was Ambrose who first articulated the concept of "just war," quoting

We hear blasphemy preached and barbarians invading. . . . How could the Roman state be safe with such defenders? . . . Plainly those who violate the faith cannot be secure. . . . Not eagles and birds must lead the army but thy name and religion, O Jesus.[4]

Just war theory was then elaborated by Augustine in the process of preaching why Christians should support Rome's resistance of the barbarians. It became the accepted means for evaluating whether the campaigns of a Christian prince were approved by Christ or not. Even today it is the chief analytical tool employed by Christian ethicists evaluating modern conflicts and by Christian preachers justifying wars to their congregations.

The last major thread in Christian ethical teaching regarding war is even more removed from the simple pacifism of Jesus, though it began with a peace campaign. In the first half of the eleventh century there was an attempt to increase the peace of Europe by promoting the concepts of the peace of God and the truce of God. War was to be permitted only at certain times, by certain persons. Holy days and holy places must be set apart for peace. Paradoxically that peace campaign helped justify Urban II's call for the first crusade or holy war. Resurrecting the Old Testament concept, Urban called the faithful to war for the peace of Jerusalem, the holiest place of all.

The idea took hold that when you fight in the right place and time for the cause of God, your fight is not only right in itself but blessed by heaven. Instead of a secular purpose circumscribed by heaven as in a just war, the crusade was ostensibly for a religious purpose. God willed the fight. From that day to this, of course, rulers and renegades have whenever possible tried to cast their battles as holy wars. In the minds of the common people, they have often succeeded. The interminable conflict between Protestants and Catholics in Northern Ireland, led largely by preachers, comes quickly to mind.

The dilemma of serious Christian ministers has always been the dilemma of applying their own understanding of Christ's teaching concerning war and peace to the particular situation in which they found themselves. On the one hand, Luther rejected the pope's crusade against the Turk. According to Bainton, Luther thought the pope the more evil of the two. His concept of the two spheres led him to argue that the church ought not be involved in the conduct of war in any case. "[The minister] may curse and damn the malefactor, but he may employ no weapons other than the Word."[5] On the other hand, the secular powers could and should resist the Turk. That was their proper place and function. Luther had no trouble preaching war for those whose role it was to conduct it.

Indeed most often preaching peace has been the practice, not of preachers of the majority, but of those whose values already ran counter to the dominant religion—"the Anabaptists in the sixteenth century, the Quakers in the seventeenth, and the Brethren in the eighteenth."[6] The majority have usually seemed to be able to find sufficient biblical reason for supporting whatever policy was convenient at the moment. In the 1930s, most Baptist preaching was both pacifist and isolationist, as were the sentiments of the country. With the coming of World War II, Baptist preachers swiftly altered their exegesis. God, they were sure, wanted the antichrist Hitler demolished. Fewer than fifty Southern Baptists registered as conscientious objectors to the war.

In Germany, ministers faced a similar dilemma. Raised on the separation of government and religious spheres, German Lutherans by and large supported Hitler. Only a relatively few, such as Dietrich Bonhoeffer, opposed the reich. Bonhoeffer put his preaching into action and was hung by the Nazis in 1945 for involvement in a plot to assassinate Hitler.

Interestingly, with regard to two issues at least, the third quarter of the twentieth century seemed to bring a change. The civil rights struggle brought a number of ministers into direct conflict with the dominant values of their congregations. A number of pastors preached pro-civil rights sermons. Some were dismissed. Some were threatened. In the free churches, especially, the lack of a church hierarchy to support a line of teaching put many parish ministers at risk. Even within the African-American community, some regarded ministers such as Martin Luther King, Jr. as dangerous troublemakers.

The Vietnam War produced similar divisions. Unpopular with large segments of the people, the Vietnam conflict created a situation in which many preachers could and did preach toward an end to the hostilities without getting themselves fired. Precisely because there was no consensus on the need for or justness of the war, ministers found room to examine such issues publicly.

Historically, most ministers seem to have worked to keep their social teaching within range of the convictions and practices of their congregations. In my first pastorate in the Bluegrass region of Kentucky, significant portions of the congregation made their living either by raising tobacco, working in the local distilleries, or breeding racehorses. They expected me to preach against smoking, drinking, and gambling! Had I pressed far into the evils of participating in such industries at any level, however, it would have been a different matter.

A cynic would say it is fine in most American congregations for ministers to preach as radically as they want, as long as that preaching is irrelevant to the actual situation of the people. Which leads us directly to the issue of AIDS ministry at First Church. How does a minister reconcile the demands of gospel living with the at-least-understandable fears and/or opposition of the people?

What biblical insights
help us develop an ethic of social action?

Any understanding of a biblical ethic of social action must begin with a look at the prophetic tradition. Biblical religion has been ethical from the very beginning. That is, it has dealt with the impact of a relationship with the divine on the actual life situation and conduct of God's people.

Old Testament prophets made it their business to speak for God to the moral and ethical failures of the people. No more dramatic example of Old Testament social prophecy exists than God's condemnation of Israel through the prophet Amos:

> Thus says the Lord: For three transgressions of Israel, and for four, I will not revoke the punishment; because they sell the righteous for silver, and the needy for a pair of sandals—they who trample the head of the poor into the dust of the earth, and push the afflicted out of the way; father and son go in to the same girl, so that my holy name is profaned. (2:6-7)

Because the everyday life of the people was so profaned, God considered their religious life profaned as well:

> I hate, I despise your festivals, and I take no delight in your solemn assemblies. Even though you offer me your burnt offerings and grain offerings, I will not accept them. . . . Take away from me the noise of your songs; I will not listen to the melody of your harps. But let justice roll down like waters, and righteousness like an everflowing stream. (5:21-24)

Old Testament prophecy thus drew a direct connection between the ethical conduct and the religious condition of the people. Not even the most exalted ritual ministries of the cultus were valid apart from genuine righteousness on the part of the people. That righteousness, moreover, was often described in specifically social terms. Oppression of the poor and needy ranks as one of the primary offenses in Amos. Sharp business practices and the failure of charity are condemned out of hand.

Jesus, as the crowning example of the prophetic tradition, continued in precisely the same vein. His picture of the last judgment in Matthew 25 gives a specifically social interpretation of his message:

> Then the king will say to those at his right hand, "Come, you that are blessed by my Father, inherit the kingdom prepared for you from the foundation of the world; for I was hungry and you gave me food, I was thirsty and you gave me something to drink, I was a stranger and you welcomed me, I was naked and you gave me clothing, I was sick and you took care of me, I was in prison and you visited me." Then the righteous will answer him, "Lord when was it? . . ." And the king will answer them, "Truly I tell you, just as you did it to one of the least of these who are members of my family, you did it to me." (vv. 34-40)

Jesus' social ethic thus differs radically from those churches that major either on liturgical ritual or pietistic conversionism. Jesus' point could be summed up by Barnette's aphorism, "There is no such thing as a personal gospel apart from a social gospel. There is but one gospel, and it is both personal and social." Truly converted people, those whose relationship with God is authentic and determinative for their lives, will be involved in helping others. That is the test of genuine conversion.

This dimension of ethical social action lies so intertwined with Jesus' teachings about the nature of our relationship with God that it cannot be separated. The commandment to "love the lord your God with all your heart, and with all your soul, and with all your strength, and with all your mind" (Luke 10:27). does not finish till it adds "and your neighbor as yourself." Indeed the Greek word often translated righteousness, *dikaiousinis*, is precisely the same word that is also translated justice. The two ideas, right relationship with God and right relationship with one's fellow human beings, are two halves of the same whole.

Paul, who was perhaps more responsible for the subsequent shape of the Christian faith than Jesus, often seems to have been more interested in theology than in social action. Even he, however, recognized the social nature of his adopted faith.

> And God is able to provide you with every blessing in abundance, so that . . . you may share abundantly in every good work. As it is written, "He scatters abroad, he gives to the poor; his righteousness endures forever." (2 Cor 9:8-9)

"Generosity" finds a place as one of the gifts of the Spirit, as does "kindness" (Gal 5:22). Teaching is third in his list of offices in the church, followed by "deeds of power, then gifts of healing, forms of assistance" (1 Cor 12:28). One is led to suspect that the everyday life of Pauline churches must have been much more involved in helping others than would appear from the majority of his writings.

It is significant, moreover, that the office of deacon, or "servant"—the first church position that appeared after the apostles—came into being for the purpose of making certain that food in the Jerusalem church was distributed fairly (Acts 6:2). The Christian impulse, then, has always been toward helping those who could not help themselves as is witnessed by the countless Christian hospitals, orphanages, and charitable enterprises that have transformed the character of Western civilization. Because that impulse has often been partially and imperfectly applied is the fault of history and culture rather than a flaw in Christian teaching itself.

We cannot leave this section, finally, without pointing out the essentially ethical character of *agape* love itself. Defined by Barnette as "to will and to work for the well being" of the one loved, *agape* itself would introduce the ethical dimension into Christianity if it were the only Christian principle we had. The apostle John helps us here,

> We know love by this, that he laid down his life for us—and we ought to lay down our lives for one another. How does God's love abide in anyone who has the world's goods and sees a brother or sister in need and yet refuses help? (1 John 3:16-17)

The implicit answer is it does not. A church or a Christian who fails to do what can be done to help those in need has placed itself outside the gospel tradition. No other conclusion can be drawn from the biblical evidence.

How do ministers pursue an ethic of social action for the church, especially in the face of opposition?

The saddest part of the vignette concerning the church's response to an HIV-positive child is that it could have been taken from numbers of newspaper accounts in communities scattered all over America. This particular issue, the issue of response to a child with a dangerous disease, is of course complicated by its association in people's minds with the controversial issue of male homosexual promiscuity. The purpose of this section is not to develop a comprehensive response to either of these issues as such. Books have been written on the subjects. My attempt here is rather to articulate why and how a minister goes about approaching any such issue.

Of course, the church is called to respond to people in need. That call is not limited by any biblical stricture I can find. It is to love and work for the well-being of all people, especially those with particular needs. Jesus' commandments to love and specifically to love others as yourself leave no option for the obedient Christian. The child Annie has to be as much an object of that church's concern and compassion as any other child in the congregation. She must not be abandoned or turned away.

To say this is not to say of course that it will be easy. Along with the compulsion to compassion, there must be a second principle observed, that of education. No minister can reasonably expect his or her people to take an enlightened position on any social action issue without proper education. Paul prayed in Philippians 1:9-10 "that your love may overflow more and more with knowledge and full insight to help you to determine what is best." He thus set the agenda for Christian ethical education.

Pastor Hall does appear to have begun dealing with the issue in the church before Annie actually arrived. The institution of universal precautions was a necessary and helpful step. Apparently, however, she did not talk about the issue and its implications enough to prepare the people, especially the parents of other children. No church should attempt to enter this kind of ministry without full discussion of its practical implications. What if Annie bites another child? What if she scrapes a knee and begins to bleed? Full information about possible dangers and procedures to cope with them should be available to every parent and preschool worker in the congregation.

In some cases, of course, social ethics directives come from denominations to pastors and churches who are then obligated to institute them. This practice has the advantage of conveying a certain authority to the minister's leadership. In practical terms, however, any minister would be foolish to attempt a potentially controversial social action effort without full discussion and preparation within the congregation. I know of an instance in my home state during the civil rights struggle in which a white pastor who preached for racial justice was punched on the jaw by a deacon on his way out of church! Nor is that by any means the worst incident of its kind.

In some cases, the minister may judge that as a result of cultural prejudices or social attitudes, a congregation is not ready to take constructive action regarding an issue. This does not excuse the minister from dealing with it. It does mean that education should begin at levels appropriate to the specific situation. Clearly the parents of other preschoolers thought Annie might be a danger to their children. They needed to be educated at the point of their fear.

A third principle to remember is that ministerial leadership on any issue of social ethics is limited by the nature and depth of the ministerial relationship that has been established with the people. This principle harks back to our "authority of servanthood" discussion in Chapter 4.

I currently serve a church in which I have been on staff a much shorter time than my colleagues. Over time they have built trust relationships with the people that I do not yet have. It would be foolish at this point in the relationship for me to attempt to lead the people with regard to a potentially divisive ethical issue. I simply have not built up the credit for people to trust me as they do my colleagues in this place. On the other hand, I have known ministers whose congregations would follow them with regard to almost any issue because of the mutual bonds of trust built up over the years.

Some congregations simply are not ready to deal with some issues of social justice that may seem obvious to their ministers. In the state of Kentucky are many congregations whose people have derived their income for generations from the raising of tobacco. It is obvious to any responsible minister that tobacco growing means participating in and benefiting from an industry that destroys the health and takes the lives of hundreds of thousands of Americans each year. But it remains highly doubtful that any minister in Kentucky tobacco country even today could successfully lead his or her people to give up growing tobacco for profit. The evil is too integral a part of the culture and too tied to positive values such as the small family farm that people cherish.

A fourth principle nonetheless suggests that ministers must maintain a sense of objectivity that allows them to evaluate clearly what their congregation's social challenges actually are. Christ's injunction to care for "the least of these" informs us here. In the city where I grew up, African-American poverty was so pervasive a part of the culture that white churches had simply ceased to see it as anything other than normative. They could not and did not help because they did not see the problem and because their ministers did nothing to help them see the problem.

In this sense the Christian minister must always be ready to act as a troubler of those who are "at ease in zion." It is admirable that ministers Armstrong and Allen had led their church to begin at least to look at the issue of AIDS-infected children and what they could do to help. That fact shows a sensitivity on their part to the needs of a group of their neighbors who might easily be overlooked. If they can handle the consequences of having moved too far too fast without adequate preparation, their congregation will be better for having addressed the issue.

Our fifth and final principle is related to the first. Christian involvement in social action is not only a matter of calling in Christ's teachings, it is also a matter of judgment. To ignore the practical social implications of the gospel in favor of an arid piety is to miss the essence of the gospel message altogether. It is to refuse to be a part of Christ's mission of redemption, which is necessarily for both this world and the next.

The Christian who undergoes a religious experience but never translates that experience into concrete ethical action for others is, in Christ's judgment, no Christian at all. Christian ministers must therefore see it as an integral part of their task to lead their people toward social action in addition to personal piety. The division of the two that is common, especially in evangelical circles in America, can only be described as the foulest heresy. It misrepresents Christ altogether.

How do I balance prophetic and pastoral concerns in preaching and church leadership in order to care for the welfare of the church body?

No one seemed to know how it had started. Everyone liked the new pastor when he came. Giving was good. Enthusiasm was high. But a year later church leaders began to recognize that things had changed. Attendance had fallen off perceptibly. The nominating committee was having trouble recruiting workers for the new church year. Giving was down. It looked as though the plans for a new family life center might stall out for lack of enthusiasm. Finally, on a Saturday morning in September, pastor and elders sat down for his yearly evaluation. They were half an hour into saying not very much when the ax fell.

"Well, Pastor, it appears to me you make the gospel too hard!" the senior elder observed. "People come to church for comfort and encouragement, and you tell us about poverty in the inner city and our failure to support the church financially. We leave feeling guilty as dirt. It's no wonder people aren't coming. We don't come here to be preached at!"

Everyone laughed nervously, but Mike knew from the looks on their faces this was what they'd come to say to him today.

That night after dinner he took a long walk to think. Could it be the elders were right? He'd been trained in an activist seminary, and he'd longed for the day when he could lead a church to be really committed to changing things in Jesus' name. Now it appeared they really didn't want to change. They just wanted him to make them feel good. Or was it fair of him to think of it this way?

Suddenly ethics class came back to mind. "The gospel is always gift and demand," Dr. Stassen was saying. "If you give a church too much gift, and not enough demand, then you'll never get anything done. But if you give them too much demand, and not enough gift, then they'll never follow where you lead."

Slowly he turned around and began to make his way toward home.

How have ministers normally dealt with their obligation for the welfare of the church?

In the previous section we looked at the impact of a particular social issue, and the minister's reaction to it, on his or her relationship with the church. In this final section of our framework for ethics in ministry, we take a step back in order to examine the minister's overall obligation for the welfare of the congregation. It is the minister's task, after all, to build up and not to destroy. In every age and place a minister is judged, if not always by numbers, then at least by the ability to create and sustain the well-being of the congregation. If that is not precisely our charge from Christ himself, then it is at least how most of us have most often understood it.

How is that done? Through the turbulent early years of the church, looking toward the development of the Roman hierarchy, the welfare of the congregation came to be seen primarily in terms of its obedience. Early in the second century, Ignatius wrote to the church at Smyrna,

> Avoid divisions as the beginning of evils. All of you follow the bishop as Jesus Christ followed the Father, and follow the presbytery as the apostles; and respect the deacons as the commandment of God.[7]

That obedience would be the hallmark of Christian church life for a millenium and a half. An individual church existed simply as the parish outpost of the universal church in that locality. Since all local residents were part of the parish, all were responsible for its well-being. While the community existed, the church existed. That, at least, was the theory of Christendom.

With the rise of religious tolerance within nations in the seventeenth and eighteenth centuries, it began to be possible for the first time for people to choose freely which congregation in an area they would attend. And thus it began to be possible for congregations to wax and wane in prosperity quite apart from the economy of their localities. People could choose a church according to the comprehensiveness of its services and the abilities of its ministers. That change had a profound effect on the development of the character of the Protestant ministry generally, and the free church ministry in particular. It introduced an objective criterion of ability into ministerial performance evaluations.

A minister who could gather a crowd and thereby produce a prosperous congregation thus came to be considered a success more than a minister who was simply an obedient child of the Church. Luther, Calvin, the Wesleys, Jonathan Edwards, and others are remembered principally because they were successful at what they did. This is not to say that those successful in building large congregations are the only ministers we remember. Some, such as the British Baptist John Bunyan and the American Quaker John Woolman, are remembered rather for their commitment to particular principles. Woolman spent his entire itinerant ministry attempting to convince individual American slaveholders to free their Africans and renounce the institution. Bunyan served more than half his adult life in prison rather than cease preaching the gospel as he understood it.

Still the success principle became an inescapable factor in the free church. As a result, churches tended more to reflect the values of their culture than to challenge those values in the name of Christ. John Lee Eighmy's *Churches in Cultural Captivity*[8] does an excellent job of portraying how one denomination, the Southern Baptists, came to accept and defend the cultural racism of their region. Simply put, the polity that allowed churches to be ruled by the laity also allowed the laity to control the social teachings of the church. In a racist culture, the church in order to exist and prosper as an institution became racist by default.

Churches that retained some measure of hierarchical structure did somewhat better in this regard than did the Baptists. Methodists and Presbyterians were able to renounce racism officially long before their Baptist kin. The Episcopal church in America never split over slavery. The issue suggests, however, something of the depth and intensity of cultural compromise that impoverishes the life of the churches with regard to a number of issues even today.

In twentieth-century America, even after more than a quarter of a century of substantial progress on civil rights, eleven o'clock on Sunday morning is still held by many to be the most segregated hour of the week. The most successful ministers are not often those who challenge their people to live lives more ethically attuned to the teachings of Christ. Most often they are those who avoid social ethics issues altogether in their preaching or who carefully attune their messages to the felt social needs and predispositions of their congregations. This is not to say that considerable Christian work regarding social ethics is not done. It is. The previous section of this chapter makes that clear. It is to say, however, that, in the average congregation today, the minister who attempts to create sensitivity to social justice issues is often swimming upstream.

Today's ministers face the problem of responsibility for both the spiritual and temporal welfare of their congregation. More than ever before, congregations today must make their way in the marketplace of ideas. More than ever before, a congregation's prosperity depends on the degree to which its ministers are able to present an interpretation of the gospel that has broad appeal. And they must somehow come to grips with the reality that those two welfares, the spiritual and the temporal, may often exist in tension and sometimes in open conflict.

What biblical insights help us in developing an ethic for ministers as responsible for the well-being of their congregations?

We have previously mentioned the Old Testament concept of *shalom*, the peace that includes peace with God and with others, well-being in the fullest sense of the term. In a sense, the *shalom* of the church is the goal of the minister. We apprehend something of that idea in the midst of the first idealism of the Jerusalem church:

> All who believed were together and had all things in common; they would sell their possessions and goods and distribute the proceeds to all, as any had need. Day by day, as they spent much time together in the temple, they broke bread at home and ate their food with glad and generous hearts, praising God and having the goodwill of all the people. And day by day the Lord added to their number those who were being saved. (Acts 2:44-47)

Frequently, of course, maintenance of that well-being requires severe measures. Peter's execution-in-the-Spirit of Ananias and Sapphira was designed to protect the integrity of that same first congregation. Clearly that must have been a sermon that got the church's attention.

Because the New Testament writers are engaged in the process of creating a social ethic which defines what it means to be church in the first place, they are seldom found to be in the position of modern ministers seeking to shape or alter the life of an already-existing institution. And yet in some cases, the New Testament writers appear to shrink from some of the ethical implications of the faith, precisely because they would be difficult to implement.

Paul's dealings with the question of slavery provide an interesting illustration. Slavery was, of course, a nearly universal institution in the ancient world. Hebrew tradition theoretically did not allow Jews to be enslaved permanently. They were to be freed at the year of Jubilee. How often this happened in practice, we do not know. We can assume that, had the first-century churches challenged the institution of slavery itself, they would have been persecuted even more severely than they were. Slavery was one of the economic cornerstones of the Roman Empire.

In that context, Paul's struggles with the issue are illuminating indeed. On the one hand, he lays down the great principle of Galatians 3:27-28.

> As many of you as were baptized into Christ have clothed yourselves with Christ. There is no longer Jew or Greek, there is no longer slave or free, there is no longer male and female; for all of you are one in Christ Jesus.

From a modern perspective, we would think that unity in Christ would make it impossible for Christians to hold slaves or support the institution. In Paul's heart, that seems to be the case. The book of Philemon represents an appeal from Paul to the Christian slaveowner Philemon on behalf of the runaway slave Onesimus, who has also become a Christian. Paul's clear intent is that Philemon forgive the runaway and free him (v. 16).

Elsewhere, however, Paul appears intent not so much to change the institution as to "humanize" and "Christianize" it:

> Slaves, obey your earthly masters with fear and trembling, in singleness of heart, as you obey Christ; not only while being watched, and in order to please them, but as slaves of Christ, doing the will of God

171

from the heart. Render service with enthusiasm, as to the Lord and not to men and women, knowing that whatever good we do, we will receive the same again from the Lord, whether we are slaves or free. And, masters, do the same to them. Stop threatening them, for you know that both of you have the same Master in heaven, and with him there is no partiality. (Eph 6:5-9)

Clearly a double standard of some kind is at work. I would argue that Paul's first priority was the peace of the church. He never thought to challenge directly an institution so universal and accepted. To do so would have invited disaster. He never said in so many words that he believed the institution wrong, but both the logical conclusion of his theological assertions and the effect of his own efforts point in that direction. For Philemon and Onesimus, Paul argued that their Christian brotherhood took precedence over their economic relationship, but as a whole he simply sought to ameliorate problems slavery created within the church.

The lens through which New Testament writers viewed their social situation was the welfare of the church. We see this again in the difference between Paul and John in their view of the secular government. In Romans 13, Paul argues strongly that the rulers get their authority from God:

Let every person be subject to the governing authorities; for there is no authority except from God, and those authorities that exist have been instituted by God. Therefore whoever resists authority resists what God has appointed, and those who resist will incur judgment. (vv. 1-2)

The Roman situation was that the church had gotten a bad name for disorderliness. Jews and Christians had been fighting one another in the streets. To the Romans, they were all Jews, and things had gotten so bad at one point that the emperor Claudius had actually expelled the Jews from Rome. Paul was arguing for good citizenship as a hallmark of the church.

By the time John wrote Revelation thirty or forty years later, though, things had changed dramatically. The empire was on the verge of a major persecution. The benevolent government that had kept the peace and made easy the early spread of the church was bent on destroying it. In the language of apocalypticism, John described the Roman government again:

The beast was given a mouth uttering haughty and blasphemous words, and it was allowed to exercise authority for forty-two months. It opened its moght to utter blasphemies against God, blaspheming his name and his dwelling, that is, those who dwell in heaven. And it was allowed to make war on the saints and to conquer them. It was given authority over every tribe and people and language and nation. (13:5-7)

The nature of the Roman government itself had not changed, but rather the government's attitude toward the church. As a result, a new generation of Christians was taught suspicion toward secular authority rather than slavish obedience to it. The key concept though is the same for both authors despite their different conclusions. They both wrote out of concern for the welfare of the church.

Did the New Testament church ever get involved in social ethics concerns simply because they were right? Of course it did. The Corinthian church built an ethic of sexual chastity and fidelity in the midst of a pagan bacchanal. The church at Ephesus condemned idolatry despite the demands of the local economy. Women in the churches were consistently regarded with dignity in the face of a culture that denied their worth. The whole thrust of New Testament morality was nothing short of revolutionary. Most often, however, in those early years the church accomplished its reforms by changing the people it converted rather than by attempting to change the society in which it found itself. Jesus' vision of a city set on a hill would wait for the day when the church grew strong enough in itself to have an impact on society as a whole.

It is important to remember, however, that Jesus saw the task of his disciples in their worlds as in many ways akin to his own efforts among the Jews. The kingdom of heaven is like a tiny mustard seed that grows to great size. It is like yeast that leavens a whole loaf. Christ's disciples are to be the light of the world. The movement toward a more aggressive interest in social ethics by the church waited only a sense of assurance regarding its own survival, coupled with the realization that the end was not to come so quickly that the world should simply be abandoned to its fate.

It is also important to remember that the New Testament writers never hesitated to correct the churches when they thought it was necessary. Second Corinthians speaks of a harsh letter from Paul that made the church at Corinth exceedingly sorry and repentant (7:5-13). The writer of the Pastoral Epistles urged Timothy to be diligent in his correction of the church.

> For the time is coming when people will not put up with sound doc-
> trine, but having itching ears, they will accumulate for themselves
> teachers to suit their own desires, and will turn away from listening to
> the truth and wander away to myths. (2 Tim 4:3-4)

As an interpreter of the gospel for the people, the minister's responsibility is to represent Christ as faithfully as he or she is capable of doing.
The responsibility for the people's relationship with Christ is ultimately
their own.

What ethical conclusions can we draw regarding a minister's responsibility for the well-being of the church?

The key concept in developing a minister's relationship with a church
lies implicit in virtually everything we have examined thus far in this
book. It is balance. Ministers are responsible to God for their care of the
well-being of the church. That well-being is to be understood in the
broadest possible sense. Spiritual well-being is certainly primary.
Everything done, taught, attempted, or corrected must be carried out
with a view to the integrity of the church's relationship to and representation of Christ.

To that end the minister's approach to the congregation should be
both nurturing and corrective, as Christ's would have been. We surmise
that Pastor Mike's approach to his congregation in his first year may
have been harsher than was necessary. Christ always approached
people with a love that was honest and an honesty that was loving.
Ministers and Christians generally seem to have a much harder time
striking the right note. Mike should have sought a greater appreciation
for the congregation's strengths before he began to attack their
weaknesses.

There does come a time when a minister feels so strongly about
some spiritual or ethical issue that he or she cannot in good conscience
fail to deal with it. Such was certainly true of both Paul and John when
they took such different positions on the Roman government. In those
cases, the approach should still be made with a view to the long-term
welfare of the congregation. John couched his condemnation of Rome
in the language of apocalypticism precisely to protect those who would
read the teaching. He made the condemnation to protect their spiritual
well-being, but he was well aware that in so doing he put them at jeapordy. Carefulness is thus always in order, whether the jeapordy to be
faced is external or internal.

Timing is also a significant factor. Paul's failure to crusade against the institution of slavery does not mean his eighteenth- and nineteenth-century children in the faith were wrong. It simply was not time yet to attack the whole institution when Paul wrote. He could not have hoped for success. What he could do was change the lot of slaves within the church, and that he did. By the time the abolitionists began their crusades, the church had done its leavening work in Western culture. The whole trend of human life was toward freedom, and that had made possible what would not have been possible before.

The temporal well-being of the church is therefore always a consideration, even with regard to clearly spiritual issues. Ministers have a responsibility to gauge carefully the potential effects of their leadership with regard to specific issues. Hindsight is frequently the only absolutely clear vision possible. Thus, when Martin Luther King, Jr. and other African-American ministers began the civil rights crusade in the 1950s, many of their colleagues opposed the effort as too dangerous. In fact, it was dangerous. Black churches were destroyed. Black ministers, and in some cases black children, were injured or killed. King and his supporters went ahead becaused they judged the issue to be larger than the welfare of any single congregation. When matters of social ethics are concerned, there will always be differences of opinion.

An insight from just war theory is useful here. One of the tenets of that theory has always been the concept of proportionality. Is the end to be achieved worth the cost? Each minister must take responsibility for gauging the possible consequences of her actions on the welfare of the church itself. Especially in the free church, the minister is not responsible alone. But he is responsible.

Part of the dynamic in Pastor Mike's yearly evaluation is a perfectly healthy respect for the wisdom of the church body itself. If he listens both to what the leaders say to him and to the intent behind their words, he may gain invaluable insight into what he has been doing, and whether and how to alter his approach. The free church concept of the "priesthood of the believer" finds particular importance when it comes to dealing with issues that may affect the health of a congregation. A minister who takes a church into confrontation on any issue without substantial support from the mature leadership of the church is not prophetic but merely foolish.

Faithful ministers will strive to remain so close to the mind and spirit of Christ that they will be confident when the moment of decision comes. Of course, the Holy Spirit must always be the ultimate guide for all the work of a minister. This is not said merely to provide a pious ending for the book. It is to remind us all that, within the limits of this present world, we seek to do the will of God. We cannot expect always to perceive that will with clarity, but we can seek God's help as we strive. And we can be confident that God will assist us and value our efforts. Luther suggested that we love God and *"Pecca fortiter!"* sin boldly! Surely there is comfort in that. In the economy of the cross, even our mistakes can be redeemed.

Notes

[1]Frank Stagg, *The Book of Acts: The Early Struggle for an Unhindered Gospel* (Nashville: Broadman Press, 1955).

[2]H. Richard Niebuhr, *Christ and Culture* (New York: Harper & Row, 1951) 39-40.

[3]Roland H. Bainton, *Christian Attitudes toward War and Peace* (Nashville: Abingdon, 1960) 53-54.

[4]Ambrose, *De Fide Christiana*, II, 16, quoted in Bainton, 90.

[5]Ibid., 139.

[6]Ibid., 136.

[7]Ignatius (c.112), *Epistle to the Smyrnaeans*, c.viii, quoted in *Documents of the Christian Church*, 2nd. ed., Henry Bettenson, ed. (London: Oxford University Press, 1963) 63.

[8]John Lee Eighmy, *Churches in Cultural Captivity; A History of the Social Attitudes of Southern Baptists* (Knoxville TN: University of Tennessee Press, 1972).

CONCLUSION

The difficulty with any ethics text is that one can never deal with all the issues. Life will always spring surprises. No minister can ever be fully prepared for all the situations he or she will encounter in parish life. Part of the intent of this book has been to suggest something of the range of issues a minister must deal with in entering into the professional practice of Christian ministry.

The larger purpose, however, has been to suggest by example a way of proceeding in making ethical decisions in ministry. This methodology will be seen by some people as a straight-line approach to ethical decisions. (You do this, and then you do this, and so on.) Others may prefer to think of it in terms of a complex of bases that should be touched, though not necessarily in a fixed order.

The concept itself is simple and can be practiced by those without extensive training in philosophical or ethical inquiry. Every Christian decision is assumed to be a decision with an authority base somewhere in Christian teaching. The minister's task is to seek to locate the appropriate authority base for each issue and bring it to bear as he or she makes decisions. As a conservative Christian (on the grand scale of things), I have chosen to locate my basis of authority in the Bible. Therefore, each ministry ethics decision is made in some fashion as follows.

One begins with trying to understand the question. What issue must be decided? How has that issue been dealt with in church history as a whole and in one's own particular denominational, cultural, and ministerial context? What insights do secular history and social sciences have to offer?

Once the issue is clearly defined, and all relevant facts are in hand, one moves to examine possible sources of authority. How have other ministers responded? What about Christian ethicists? What biblical principles inform the situation or decision called for?

Since biblical principles are paramount for me, these alone may sometimes determine much of the shape of a particular response. For the Christian, however, there is also always the more mystical element of the impetus of the Holy Spirit. One assumes that, given time, a Christian minister will pray about ministry decisions and seek the guidance of the Holy Spirit in making them.

Finally, however, one must decide a course of action, plan it, and carry it out. This course of action may then be altered as experience teaches. The minister who never alters an ethical choice on the basis of experience and feedback simply is not paying attention.

This ethical method is essentially that taught by Henlee Barnette for many years at the Southern Baptist Theological Seminary. Its great advantage lies in its accessibility to thoughtful Christians with or without extensive ethical training. Other methods are more sophisticated, but this one can shed light on virtually any significant ethical issue if carefully applied.